ATLANTIS

Carlo & Renzo Piano

ATLANTIS

A JOURNEY IN SEARCH OF BEAUTY

*Translated from the Italian
by Will Schutt*

Europa
editions

Europa Editions
8 Blackstock Mews
London N4 2BT
www.europaeditions.co.uk

Translation by Will Schutt
Original title: *Atlantide. Viaggio alla ricerca della bellezza*
Translation copyright © 2020 by Europa Editions

A catalogue record for this title is available from the British Library
ISBN 978-1-78770-261-5

Piano, Carlo & Renzo
Atlantis

Book design by Emanuele Ragnisco
www.mekkanografici.com

Cover image: © Renzo Piano, Design Emanuele Ragnisco

Prepress by Grafica Punto Print – Rome

Printed and bound in Great Britain by Clays Ltd, Elcograf S.p.A.

CONTENTS

To all those
looking for Atlantis

ATLANTIS

Text Carlo Piano in Simoncini Garamond
Text Renzo Piano in Helvetica

1.
MACAIA

A long sea. So long and lazy it darkens your thoughts and makes your stomach churn, while low-lying clouds dissolve in water. Up seems down. The few drafts of air are hot and full of moisture. Back home we'd say the sirocco was blowing; I don't know what they say around here. I do know that in Croatia they call this wind *jugo* and in Libya *ghibli*. Often yellow with the sands of Africa, it scatters the dust of the desert far and wide.

Everything around us is still, except for the long waves. Our latitude is 7°18'36" South, our longitude 72°24'16" East. We're in the middle of nowhere, in the heart of the Indian Ocean, off the coast of the Chagos Islands, which I had never heard of before. For military reasons, we cannot land. So secret are the army bases that fifty years ago all of the inhabitants were deported to Mauritius, never to return. They still protest.

I wonder by what twist of fate I've boarded this ship traveling away from the world I know at nine knots an hour. I wonder what my father is doing here, looking from the upper deck at the murky line between the sky and the sea, a line swallowed up by the surreal haze of *macaia*.

He rests his elbows on the railing and looks out at the ocean, the one view available. He is measuring the length of the waves with his eyes. Measure, measure, measure—he's obsessed. In his tattered right pocket, he keeps a yellow roll-up tape measure, which he regularly uncoils. He also attempts to guess distances and weights, a kind of personal challenge.

In my opinion these waves have a period of one hundred meters and are three meters high. The long waves come from far away, from all the waters further east: the Andaman Sea, Pulau Nias, Sumatra, Java, the Sunda Strait. A wave is pure energy, rising from one point and propagating through space and time. In reality, it is pure momentum. It carries nothing on its back.

I like measuring these long waves. To measure is to gesture towards knowledge, to attempt to understand. My friends call me the "Surveyor," but I don't just survey the land. I also measure the many angles and points of the sea, too. I measure everything. Things and distances.

The extraordinary engineer Peter Rice and I used to bet on the dimensions of things all the time: the diameter of a table, the speed of a train, the depth of a lake. Whoever guessed closest won.

One thing about getting into the habit of making measurements in your head is that you end up imagining not only what you see but the invisible forces at work: torsion, inertia, and the effects of the wind, heat, cold, and earthquakes.

Fortunately, hidden in the hull of this 170-metric-ton ship is a gyroscope, which makes the ship more stable. Keeps it from rolling. Do you know how a gyroscope works? It's a rotational device that, owing to the law of conservation of angular momentum, tends to maintain its axis of rotation in a fixed direction . . .

I have a vague idea about what a gyroscope is, but the waves are a total mystery. Researchers say some waves roam the ocean for more than a century before crashing into a cliff or splashing against a pier covered with mollusks. Could that be true? If so, then no one, not even my father, can say for certain where these waves come from. If they are a century old, they could be the same that swallowed, say, the ocean liner *Principessa Mafalda* off the coast of Brazil. Or carried messages in bottles at the turn of the twentieth century. There are all kinds of waves: transverse waves, square waves, breaking waves, barrel or cyclic waves. They can be spectacular and thunderous or insignificant and deceptively harmless. In this sliver of the Indian Ocean, the waves are especially long and unpleasant. My father can't stand them. I can barely stand them. *Macaia* changes people's personalities, darkens even the most cheerful among us.

There is another mystery that troubles me: what color is the sea? When we're young we're convinced it's blue or azure. Nonsense. It's daubed with turquoise, indigo, gray, green, emerald, and pure see-through. When it's overcast it's gunmetal, in the dark it's black, at sunrise and sunset it appears flecked with gold. Sometimes there are whitecaps. Winds affect the color: the sirocco turns it silver, the tramontane glass. For Homer, it became the color of wine at dusk, but I'm not so sure I trust him. They say he was blind.

The truth is the color of the sea is undefinable. No one knows what color it is. Every wave has its own, different light. My father can measure them all he wants, but in my opinion waves will always elude mathematical models.

On days like today, when there is *macaia*, the sounds of the ocean are muffled. Detecting them is a struggle. The caws of seagulls fade and the winds become at most a murmur. All you hear is the splash of water against the hull and the thrum of the 1500-horsepower diesel engines. *Macaia* is a motionless and metaphysical haze, inside and out, a weird weather condition that often occurs off the coast of Genoa. The sirocco blankets the sky with clouds, creating a dreamlike atmosphere. Time stops, movements dwindle, the mood grows melancholic. Technically known as advection fog, *macaia* forms when moist air passes over cold ground, but for those who live in the Mediterranean, *macaia* is a fog that descends and makes your heart ache.

Some say the name *macaia* derives from the Greek word *malakia*: a languor that afflicts body and soul. Others trace it back to Arabic and others still to the Latin word *malacia*, which means, among other things, "apathy." Greek, Italian, Genoese, Arabic, Venetian—in the great lake of the Mediterranean, words, like cultures, mix, overlap, trade places. One language isn't enough to describe all the wonders of the sea.

There must be something in the chemical makeup of salt that chases off happy thoughts. Some people claim that the sea is the dwelling place of what we have lost, what we had wished for, our broken dreams, grief, and spilt tears.

The Measurer

Sailing is slowness and silence. Aboard a boat you lower your voice and look up at the sky. When he was still a kid, my father built a sailboat by hand in his garage in Pegli. He was sure he had correctly measured the garage door, but in order to get the boat out he had to demolish the wall. According to family lore, my grandpa became livid. Maybe that triggered my father's mania for measurement.

Sailing changes the rhythm of life as it is lived on firm ground. The way you walk, the way you think, the way you talk. The terminology is bizarre: "the stern," "the bow," "downwind," "upwind," "keel over," "drift leeward." You have to be more cautious, something you tend to forget when you first board. As soon as my father boards a ship he writes TAKE CARE NOT TO GET HURT in green marker on a Post-it, which he posts in plain view. If you don't slow down, a broken foot is the least you can expect. You can even fall down a hatch. I once fell a few meters and landed in the bathroom, but I was a kid at the time, with flexible bones.

On a ship there is quiet, a sense of respite, a state of suspension. The experience is as psychological as it is physical, since you're buoyant, lulled by gentle movements. And not so gentle.

*

Macaia, this tedious roll while everything around you is at a standstill, makes you nauseated. Any chance of a fresh, northerly breeze? A good close-hauled heel, sitting leeward to run your hand over the water?

For me, traveling by boat is enchanting. You experience slowness, silence, suspension. You fly and float, but you never touch the ground.

The sea makes us question many things, our sense of the horizon most of all, which is shattered by the incline, especially in rough water. However solid, the deck of a ship is not the same as dry land. Your feet acquire more importance, because you rely on them to keep your balance. Some believe that, on a buoyant surface, our feet are elevated to the status of a sense organ, on par with our hands, eyes, ears, mouth, and nose. Your feet can't get distracted and can't relax. When there's dead calm, everything is easier; the deck is almost level. But today there isn't dead calm, there's *macaia*.

Sandcastles

My father used to take us sailing every summer: me, my mother Magda, my brother Matteo, and my youngest sister Lia. Lia was very young at the time. We would make a night crossing to Corsica, which remained under Genoese control until the Treaty of Versailles. It was as if we never left territorial waters.

At dawn in the cockpit we watched the silhouette of Cap Corse emerge, the bare rugged peaks of the sierras. The wind never lets up in those parts, and Genoese watchtowers, built to fend off Saracen pirates, still stand. As we rounded the cape, the water thundered against the prow. I think it was the vacation's way of welcoming us. I enjoyed diving with my spear-gun to hunt for octopuses off the reefs. Underwater, through my mask, even a musky octopus loomed large, like a creature from the deep. I never succeeded in catching one, which may be why I enjoyed it so much.

Usually we slept in the roadstead and avoided the ports, except to restock the pantry. A necessary operation, given how few fish we caught. The stability of the earth was a mirage. "A boat is made to be on water," my father repeated, *ad nauseam*. A statement so obvious it was impossible to deny. With me came the Architect, Matteo, and Lia. On those rare occasions that we got to go to the beach, we would build sandcastles.

My father would tell us that the first thing to bear in mind was that sandcastles serve no purpose. Building sandcastles is not a war game. It's a game with the waves, an end in itself. We would look for the right spot in the sand and watch the surf on the shoreline break into white foam and retreat. We would watch for a solid quarter hour.

First thing you do is stand on the shoreline, at the edge of the beach, and observe the rise and fall of the surf. The relationship between the sandcastle and the sea is more important than it appears. Study the waves closely, one by one, then decide where to build the castle. But be careful: too close and the water will immediately destroy it, too far and the castle won't compete with the waves.

It sounds complicated, but it's actually simple and intuitive. Then dig a shallow moat with your hands, being mindful to dig where the sand is damp; make a pile; and sculpt it until you've formed the base of the castle. Ideally, the mound should sit at a forty-five degree slope. The moat need be no deeper than thirty centimeters and no wider than forty-five centimeters, whereas the castle should be sixty centimeters tall.

Now as then, all these angles, centimeters, and fluid dynamics confuse me. You're never too old to build sandcastles: it can be fun for adults, since sandcastles help us think like children. But my father isn't done with his lesson.

Afterward dig an opening in the moat to let the water in. The moment the waves first enter and flood the moat is magical. If the castle is in a good spot, you can watch the water run its course. Then, to store the image in your memory, close your eyes as the water arrives, quickly, before it slips away. You have to freeze the moment; your retina snaps a photograph. Then top the castle with a flag, or whatever is lying around on the beach, so that it will be visible to people walking by. Turn home and don't look back.

Don't turn around because the castle is bound to disappear, and to see it crumble would only bring disappointment. You're better off preserving the memory.

2

A Letter from Admiral Temptation

I think the time has come to explain what we're doing aboard a ship cutting through the placid surface of the Indian Ocean, though honestly I myself don't get it. But I can recount the events that brought us here. A combination of long-held desires and recent opportunities. Everything came together, as if our stars were aligned. I can't be sure, not yet at least, that this alignment is a good thing, but it is safe to say I never would have imagined crossing the Pillars of Hercules, circumnavigating Africa, like Vasco da Gama rounding the Cape of Good Hope, and crossing a sea I had not known, surrounded by the unnerving calm of *macaia*.

Our journey originated a month ago, on a day I happened to be at my father's studio, in Punta Nave. Punta Nave is named after Scoglio Nave, a smattering of rocks off the coast of Vesima, on the west side of Genoa. During the warm season boys crowd Scoglio Nave and show off to bored-looking girls by performing twists, splits, cannonballs, and tucks. In winter, on the other hand, the ledge is pummeled by waves and lashed by winds, the favorite target of the Mediterranean *mascun*. In Genoese, "*mascun*" means a slap in the face, but in Italian "*mascone*" is the word for the side of the bow, the part most exposed to breakers. This is, to put it plainly, where waves come to die. They either crash into this spur of rock or harmlessly lap its edges. Why is a mystery.

There are some secrets that the sea guards jealously: dolphin-riding nereids, phantom ships, the island of Robinson

Crusoe, pirate treasure, sirens, and the Invincible Armada, which turned out not to be so invincible. I almost forgot—the *Titanic*. "Gentleman, it has been a privilege playing with you tonight."

How many shipwrecks are lying on the ocean floor? According to some estimates there are more sunken boats than boats cruising the surface. The sea has been collecting carcasses for millennia, and according to UNESCO over three million are scattered across our oceans. Over time they become part of the landscape. Fish build their habitats inside them. Their hulls are covered with sea grass and mussels, like abandoned houses overgrown with vines. Thirty years ago, just off the coast in front of us, the oil tanker *Haven* sank. It is still lying at the bottom of this sea, about forty fathoms deep. It is inhabited by conger eels, bogues, anchovies, snappers, banded seabream, moray eels, barracudas, damselfish, gilthead bream, and blennies. Plus sponges, lobsters, oysters, anemones, corals, marine worms, and a sampling of nudibranchs. Nudibranchs are trained in the art of camouflage and hard to spot. *Haven*'s destiny was written in its name. In fact, the fish aren't disturbed by fishermen, since the place has become a marine reserve.

Though not a sea creature, my father also chose the Ligurian coast for a haven. There you'll find a foundation for young architects, his studio, and his home, where he retires in moments of silence or after a quarrel. The foundation is an old pink villa overlooking the gulf, while the other two buildings are tucked between the mountains and the sea. The buildings cling to slopes that farmers, by a heroic effort, once wrested from nature's grip. It was in his studio—suspended between earth, water, and sky—when I first heard my father utter the name Atlantis.

But I think the idea had been swirling around in his head for some time. Like everyone else, I know that Atlantis is the legendary lost city that, somewhere, at some point in time, sank into the ocean. As a young man, I read about Captain Nemo exploring the remnants of the city in Jules Verne's *Twenty Thousand Leagues under the Sea*. Nemo describes ruined temples, broken columns, petrified wood, and a volcano that spews lava underwater. More than any other imaginary land, perhaps, Atlantis has piqued the interest of philosophers, scientists, pioneers, novelists, and suckers. And now architects of certain renown.

At Punta Nave everything speaks of the sea, its backdrop, which is constantly changing in shape and appearance. I like the water, because it's lawless.

The Shunji Sea

The Japanese architect Shunji Ishida has worked with my father for over forty years, from the very beginning, since Beaubourg, or the Centre Pompidou. One day, honeymooning in Genoa with his wife Sugako, his car broke down, and he hasn't left since. My maternal grandmother Elsa rented him a spare room, with a view of the sea from the window, in her apartment in Pegli. Every morning, at the same hour and from the same angle, Shunji photographs the Mediterranean in front of the studio. Of thousands of photos no two are the same.

All the water surrounding Punta Nave must be to blame for my father's burning desire for Atlantis. Maybe Atlantis has always hounded him. After all, what does an architect dream of if not the perfect city? He chased after it in the middle of the Pacific, on the banks of the Thames and the Seine, in San Francisco's Golden Gate Park, on the islands of Japan. Stubbornly searched in Berlin when Berlin still bore the scars of the Wall, in Athens, in New York after the Twin Towers attack. He has sought perfection, but has he ever found it?

Maybe everything we do—write, build, travel the world—is just a pale imitation of what we have in mind.

But there is a specific event, a letter actually, that kindled his craving for adventure. I caught a glimpse of the letter on his desk before he buried it under a ream of sheets and sketches. It came from an old friend and shipmate, an admiral in the Italian Navy, whom we'll call Admiral Temptation. My father let it sit there for a long time, must have thought on it for months before responding. And before revealing its contents to me. Admiral Temptation was proposing a long journey by sea, what the ancients called a periplus. They would visit many ✔ places, including places where my father had built. The purpose of the mission was to update the nautical maps and pilot books for the Italian Navy's Hydrographic Institute, but there would also be time to explore.

His friend would not be taking part in the expedition, because he was busy rescuing migrant ships setting out from the northern coast of Africa to reach Europe by the Strait of Sicily. He was in charge of coordinating the Italian patrol boats that intervene to prevent shipwrecks. But Admiral Temptation wanted someone he could trust on board and swore that my father could have a say in tracing the route and choosing which depths to plumb and where to drop anchor. I wonder if that trust was well placed. I wonder because, in part, I know my father has different aspirations; he couldn't care less about cartography and has it in his head to discover whether, in some corner of the ocean that no one has ever penetrated, he'll find Atlantis.

The Circle

In the end my father accepted. Perhaps he secretly hoped to solve the mystery of the sunken city. Many minds before him had been captivated by Atlantis, not all of them irrational. Apparently, the search for lost perfection tugs at people's heartstrings. Maybe the Surveyor had a premonition he wasn't telling me about. Maybe, now that he was turning eighty, he wanted, in his way, to close that circle. For his entire life he had believed that a spirit of adventure was the essence of being an architect, hence weighing anchor became almost a moral obligation.

Then and there I didn't rule out his intentions to embark on the trip simply because he loved the sea. The view from Punta Nave lures people away with promises of flights and discoveries. I was probably embellishing, and he was just a stubborn old man. But I couldn't let him go alone: if it was Atlantis he was after, be it a myth or his own burning desire, I would go with him.

I didn't know what vessel we'd be sailing. I didn't even know if the route had been planned. Given all the bodies of water in the world, the possibilities were endless. Seen from space, Earth is a blue sphere held together by saltwater, a vast liquid mirror reflecting back the world. How long would our journey last? Six months, a year, five years? No one could say. In Genoa there's an old adage: Shipping out to war, say a prayer. Shipping out to sea, say at least two.

I still hadn't been told when or where we'd depart from. All my father told me was that he needed time to make arrangements and allocate responsibilities. Yet I came to realize this was quite serious for him. Whenever Ishmael, in *Moby-Dick*, feels the damp, drizzly November in his soul, he too escapes to the sea.

3.
REFLECTIONS BY THE PORT

Finally, the day came, a Monday in early September.

My father was waiting for me at the Calata degli Zingari. In Genoa, "*calate*" are those stretches of the dock protected by wharfs, where longshoremen and cranes load and unload cargo with varying degrees of exertion. They are often named after Fascist colonies: Benghazi, Massawa, Mogadishu, Tripoli. What distinguishes them from other docks is that they lie parallel to the coast and are shielded by perpendicular piers, so the water is calm. They're a godsend for unloading cargo ships.

We found ourselves in the Port of Genoa, and from there we would set out on our periplus, which, so the Surveyor secretly hoped, would lead us to the lost city of Atlantis. I wasn't convinced it was a good idea, not in the slightest.

Two things about the port come as a surprise. First, everything is buoyant; stillness does not reign as on dry land. Here, every object is in constant motion. Second, the bay is a vast mirror. It reflects the austere *palazzi*, passing clouds, the Lighthouse of Genoa, the boats, and the fishermen casting their lines. It must have once reflected the galleys setting out for the Battle of Meloria, the thousand sunburnt faces of sailors, the crusaders who set sail for the Holy Land led by Guglielmo Embriaco.

One wharf still commemorates the enterprise, Ponte Embriaco, by the "flying" canopy of Piazza delle Feste, which my father designed for the 1992 Genoa Expo. This water must have also captured the reflections of Paganini, Montale, and

Christopher Columbus—first as a young boy and later as an émigré returning from Spain. Their profiles must be recorded and stored somewhere in the great archive of the sea, which maybe one day we'll find a way to decode.

Peacoat

That moment on the waterfront put us in the archive too. Though it wasn't cold yet, my father was wrapped in a peacoat, the spitting image of a sea dog.

We killed time on the old piers, in the thick salty air, where container ships were tied up, their decks stacked with containers, like Lego bricks. I wondered where they were going, where they had come from. Exotic places, I imagined, stormy seas, flat oceans, and men battling homesickness. Seafaring folk: captains, cooks, cabin boys, telegraphers, salty officers. All traveling, hovering in the wind, on the waves, and in solitude. Which, by their nature, is their favorite companion.

The crusty cargo ships bespoke piracy in the Horn of Africa and called to mind winds—the libeccio, the *burazza*, the *bura*, the *greco*, the ostro, and the *baliverna*. Then the trade winds, monsoons, the khamsin blowing across the Nile Delta, the pampero whistling on the Río de la Plata. And scents, spices in the pantry, the engine room where even breathing is a struggle.

The Surveyor sat on a bollard. Leaning on bollards that have been worn and scarred by mooring lines is a normal pastime for those who hang around the waterfront. Their wear and tear make them reliable proof of a pier's age and witnesses to what has unfolded in a harbor, where only a couple things ever happen: things arrive and depart, dock and sail away.

A group of seagulls danced overhead and over the fishing boats towing their hauls from Punta Chiappa. My father decided to speak.

*

The port is and always has been a place for the exotic. A part of the world comes to find you at home. Here there arrive bits of Japan, Russia, the Philippines, or Korea.

Can you read the names on the ships? They're written in Cyrillic, Greek, Chinese, Arabic, and languages unknown. The whole world is on the move.

Ships aren't made to sit idle at the dock. They're made to transport people and cargo. Just stop and have a look: the world rushes by before you. My father on the other hand was insisting we board the Italian Navy research vessel. There was no point in replying that the underwater empire was a legend made up by Plato. An underwater oasis, bigger than Libya and Asia put together, that sank into the sea—really? He wouldn't listen to reason. To him, the idea was not preposterous. As proof, he would cite the theory of continental drift: in the course of such a process, a hundred Atlantises may have risen and fallen. My father, who from here on out we shall also call the Explorer, wanted to discover it, and his desire trumped all doubts and uncertainties.

We had already been to the Port Authority in Palazzo San Giorgio to notarize our travel documents. Above the door of the sacristy—once the Bank of San Giorgio—is an inscription: *Ubi ordo deficit nulla virtus sufficit*. Where order fails, no virtue avails. Housed inside was the Republic of Genoa's treasury: ducats, gold *genovini*, *quartarole*, silver *ottavini*, *scudi del sole*, *testoni*, *petachine*, and *cavallotti*.

Granddad's Giardinetta

But my father was elsewhere, rewinding the clock, inspired by the scent of freshly baked focaccia drifting through the port. On every corner you can find a café, more like a greasy spoon. The sailor's special is a glass of white wine and *fugassa*, Genoese focaccia.

The Port of Genoa used to be entirely different. When I was a kid my father, your grandfather Carlo, would take me to mass every Sunday and then down to the port.

Back then there were no containers. To load a bale on a ship, longshoremen would hoist it in the air on hooks and let it fly, and the ships, buoyant in the water, seemed to fly too. Cars were lifted on cranes, and cows in sling straps mooed in terror, their legs dangling in the air.

One time the longshoremen loaded your grandfather's Giardinetta onto a ferry bound for Sardinia. Back then ships didn't have ramps. We were going on holiday for the summer. They lay a net on the ground and placed the car in the middle, then attached the four corners of the net to a crane and lifted the Giardinetta off the ground. The car had wood paneling, which was then in vogue.

The ropes began to quiver as the car was hoisted in the sky. From below I caught my first glimpse of its muffler, crossbow, transaxle, and steering arms. I had the sensation I was discovering something new, defying the forces of gravity, witnessing the miracle of levitation that took place nowhere else but the port.

I seem to be rereading the story of Selim, the elephant that made landfall in Genoa, as told by Maurizio Maggiani in *The Unadorned Queen*. Selim, still in a daze from the bromide-laced forage he'd been fed, was harnessed to a cargo boom and lowered to the ground. Longshoremen and people with time on their hands packed the wharf to see the spectacle of the poor pachyderm. When Selim's four feet touched the ground without kicking up so much as a grain of dust, the crowd erupted in applause. Back in my grandfather's day, there was a famous crane operator in the port nicknamed Pellicula; watching this gravity-defying juggler man his machine was indeed like going to the movies. Pellicula could swipe the hat off an unsuspecting victim without mussing his hair. With its cast of characters, its rituals, its morals softened by the salt spray, the port has always been a parallel world.

Defying Gravity

I think the idea for building Il Bigo, my father's seven-armed crane with a panoramic lift over the Porto Antico, came from watching my grandfather Carlo's Giardinetta gently rising into the sky. I believe it was a Fiat 500, the one with rear-hinged doors. Everything in my father's memory is magnified by the imagination of a child who, every Sunday, would gape at the pageantry of the port. His father was also there, every inch the Genoese, always clenching an unlit pipe between his teeth, so that he almost never spoke. But in the 1950s, facing the wonders of the port, there was no point in talking.

Those sensations have settled like dust inside the Explorer, one layer deposited on top another. Maybe that was when his heroic struggle against the force of gravity began. Ever since he discovered gravity exists, the first time he scraped his knees. But the tie that binds them chafes; they collaborate and they do battle.

When you're building, the force of gravity helps because it holds everything together. It's a question of weight and stress; in fact, we say one builds "stone on stone." In India an architect would sit in the middle of a construction site and with a long stick indicate where exactly the workers should place the pieces. He'd spend all day at the site with them.

If you are building an arch instead of a wall, that changes things, for an arch isn't made simply by putting one piece on top of another, but by pushing together contrasting pieces. Though it is still the force of gravity that holds them together. Building a vaulted structure is even more complicated: Brunelleschi built the cupola of Florence's Santa Maria del Fiore in a spiral pattern, gradually narrowing the intervals as he reached the top. He, too, took advantage of the force of gravity, the weight, the contrasting force between stones.

Problems arise when you reach the top and have to close the structure, because the last stones aren't supported by the force of gravity. On the contrary, gravity causes them to fall. Nothing is holding them up. Look at how they solved the problem of the Pantheon in Rome. It breathes.

Building stone by stone is a work of patience as well as a work of knowhow. You proceed stone by stone. The stones cannot be used as they are in nature. You have to adapt them and work them in such a way that they support one another. In seismic zones, where the ground is moving, weight becomes a big problem. The force of gravity holds things together, but if the earth shakes, the center of gravity shifts, and that spells trouble.

Building is heavy by nature. That is why making it light, disobeying the laws of gravity, is a feat of daring. Stuck using bulky materials, a builder seeks lightness. That is why he envies sounds and words, the materials of musicians and writers, which are swift and light.

Plato

From their posts, the customs agents were scrutinizing us. Our aimlessness must have struck them as suspicious, since everyone else at the docks hustles about. Maybe they mistook us for smugglers, smuggling being a regular practice around the piers. Many sailors consider it a means of supplementing one's income, not a crime. At the Monastery of the Virgin of Montserrat, there is an ex-voto bearing the inscription: "Offered by a captain devoted to the Blessed Virgin as thanks for enabling him to smuggle for nine years without ever being fined by customs agents."

Ships kept coming and going. Someone was waving his beret from the aftercastle of an oil tanker. Greeting strangers is part of the ritual of sailing. My father removed a torn page, folded in four, from Plato's *Timaeus*. Setting his glasses on the tip of his nose, he began to read.

> [T]here was an island in front of the strait which, I've heard you say, your people call the Pillars of Heracles. The island was bigger than both Asia and Libya combined, and travellers in those days used it to get to the further islands, from where they had access to the whole mainland over on the other side, the mainland which surrounds that genuine sea. Everything this side of that strait is like a narrow-mouthed harbor, but that is the true sea, and the land which completely surrounds it truly deserves the name "mainland."[1]

Atlantis is first mentioned in Plato's dialogues, *Timaeus* and *Critias*, though *Critias* ends just as it promises to reveal more information. Apparently, beyond the Straits of Gibraltar lay a prosperous, powerful utopia. Its inhabitants, the children of Poseidon, were frank and honest people. They amassed virtues, not material goods. But with the passing of time their godliness was overshadowed by human nature. They fell from grace.

[1] Plato, *Timaeus and Critias*, translated by Robin Whitfield (Oxford World's Classics, 2008)

Plato describes how they strayed from the path of the right-eous to the path of the greedy and power-hungry. As punish-ment, Zeus battered the island with tsunamis and cataclysms, and, in the course of a day and a night, Atlantis sank.

Many have taken Plato's words at face value, not all of them mystics or quacks. The brilliant likes of Bacon, Darwin, Descartes, Pliny, and Voltaire, who identified Atlantis with the island of Madeira, took an interest in the story.

Like other legendary lands, Atlantis inspired travelers who failed to find it yet made other discoveries in the process. Many, including Columbus, departed for mythic regions and found lands that did in fact exist. Not the ones they went searching for, but others, which deepened human knowledge and, what's more, filled the coffers of their kings.

The Double

Watching some ferries slip their knots and others enter the port, the images double. Water reflects and multiplies what we see. And when it is a mirror as calm as this bay, the image turns crystal clear.

Odd that in a place as rough as this, a place to get your hands greasy, there exist such tricks of light, which render things beautiful. Strange that a port, so like a factory, exudes poetry. As Joseph Brodsky wrote (referring to Venice, but the essence is the same), "Water . . . provides beauty with its dou-ble. By rubbing water, this city improves time's looks, beauti-fies the future."

As the last rays of the sun cast shadows over the jetty, we waited for the research vessel to arrive from La Spezia. It was only 52 miles away; we wouldn't have to wait long. We passed the time by chatting.

The port is never static, constantly in motion; a fantastic imaginary city of buildings that float.

A moment ago it was different, and in ten minutes it'll change again, once this cruise ship departs and another boat takes its place. What if Captain Ahab's whaler, the *Pequod*, were to dock here? All these names make up the topography of a city that changes by the day, the hour, with cargo ships as tall as buildings coming and going. Water, saltwater, envelops the world and holds it together.

The more I thought about it, the more this dream of chasing Atlantis seemed like a nightmare. Plato's island was just a metaphor to illustrate his political theories. If Atlantis really existed, it would have already been found. Some believe it is located in the Azores, others in the Sahara. Over centuries the lost city has moved everywhere from the Antarctic to Palestine to Scandinavia to Sardinia. There are people who point to the Island of Thera, which actually did sink after a volcanic eruption in the sixteenth century B.C. Others link Atlantis to the Bermuda Triangle, where, they say, multiple airplanes and ships have disappeared. The electromagnetic storms responsible for the disappearances are, supposedly, caused by the ruins.

However attractive, these stories are, in my opinion, fantasies that fuel irrational minds. And some people, banking on their family name, have tried to exploit them to pull off major scams. In 1924 Paul Schliemann, grandson of the archaeologist who discovered Troy, claimed to have inherited documents that led to Atlantis, but it turned out that he had made it all up to line his own pockets. He may not even have been related to the famous archaeologist.

I could not believe that my father was convinced of its existence. Maybe he was looking for his own private Atlantis. Deep down, perhaps in a corner of our souls we rarely search, lies something that consumes us. A regret, a desire, a passion, what could have been and never was. Unattainable perfection, an Atlantis to pursue. Or maybe he just wanted to sail.

Water and Stone

Wherever he has gone, he has taken Genoa with him. His architectural language conjures ports, bodies of water, cargo ships, the light reflected off the sea in Southern Italy. Beaubourg looks like an outsize boat run ashore, the Whitney like a vessel floating above Manhattan, the Shard the mast of a clipper ship racing from the Indies to the Thames.

This city has a frail body and a strong soul that ranges over the world. The historian Fernand Braudel wrote that Genoa is wedged between a sea too deep and mountains too tall. He used to say that throughout its history Genoa has been a seismograph, registering every tremor. I met Braudel, arguably the greatest Mediterranean scholar, during the 1992 Expo; he knew Genoa better than the Genoese.

Genoa is a city of stone and water. This dual nature might seem like a contradiction. Its historic center encircled and shielded by stone. Its port promising adventure at sea. Genoa is a city that leaves a deep impression.

It is a casbah, a noble casbah. Its *carruggi* (alleys) ascend toward the mountains and turn, all of a sudden, impossibly steep. There is rock and then, just offshore, the deep sea. You go from the weight of stone to the ethereal nature of water. This idea of the stone city has inspired poets from Montale to Caproni. "Genoa of iron and air," writes Caproni, "my chalkboard, my sandstone."

The city cannot help but be parsimonious, a virtue that comes from its distant past and its geographic location. Its topography teaches the city to let nothing go to waste. That is by no means the same as stinginess. "*Chì nù se straggia nìnte*" is the saying that best encapsulates the Genoese. We let nothing go to waste here.

The sandstone city stretches out behind the port, from Caricamento to Commenda di Prè, in a maze of curiously populated alleys, the infamous *carruggi*. Some of their names refer to trades: Vico degli Indoratori (Street of the Gilders), Vico dei Librai (Street of the Booksellers), Salita Pollaiuoli (Street of the Poultrymen). Other streets attest to sacred and profane love: Vico dell'Amor Perfetto (Street of Perfect Love) and Vico delle Carabraghe (Pants Off Street), lined with brothels. There is also an alley called Vico delle Monachette (Street of the Young Monks), which, according to the yellow tape of the Surveyor, an authority in the field, is just seventy-nine centimeters wide. You have to squeeze through.

The *carruggi* are crammed with tall, narrow, medieval houses abutting noble palaces that modestly hide their wealth behind sober doors. More than from the sun, the shutters serve to shield the house from prying eyes. Genoa doesn't like to show off; its beauty is evasive. It is a slate quarry.

Limpets

Italo Calvino claimed that the Genoese fall into one of two groups: those who cling to the cliffs, like limpets, and those who cannot wait to take off. The Explorer belongs, without a doubt, to the latter. For him it is better to risk getting lost than to have never left. In fact, he was growing eager to board the ship, though he still hadn't told me where we were headed.

If you grow up looking out at the sea, as I did, you grow up wishing for escape. Not that I don't love Pegli; it's the suburb where I was born. But those long strolls back and forth, with the sea always there in front of us, both going and coming back, nurtured my desire to discover the world.

Genoa, the city of sailors who, as soon as they docked, would escape large open spaces and seek shelter in the stones of the alleys and smaller piazzas.

The port is open while the city is introverted, almost intimate. Yet the two live side by side on this narrow spit of land. Did the Genoese turn Genoa into a fortress, or is it Genoa that made the Genoese so reserved?

Clearly the city has forged a distinct identity. Despite years of its inhabitants crisscrossing the globe, Genoa has lost neither its spirit nor its singsong. It is a hodgepodge of languages and cultures: European, Middle Eastern, North African. The word *camallo* (longshoreman) comes from the Arabic word *hammal* (a person employed to carry things). As one saying has it, "*C'è di tutto come a Zena.*" There's a bit of everything, just like in Genoa. A testament of sorts not just to the city's frugality but to its diversity.

The city is cosmopolitan, by vocation and necessity. It has been multiethnic for centuries and derives its strength from having mixed blood.

In the city's museums you won't find one family portrait that doesn't depict every shade of skin color. Like the façade of the Cathedral of San Lorenzo, which is made of fragments from all over the world.

Truth is, as the years have gone by, my father has begun to feel like a limpet too. He didn't want to hear it, but I told him so anyway. It must come down to roots, their hold on us. One could object that his conduct tells another story: you would never find a limpet impatiently scanning the horizon. Yet when all is said and done, roots and adventures do not stand in opposition to one another. The Explorer pulled his peacoat tighter and popped the collar. Even at the end of summer, there is a chill on the wharf when the sun goes down.

See, when it comes to roots you risk building rhetorical castles in the air.

But that doesn't happen if your childhood is lived deeply and honestly, if you face your fears with passion, if your desires are excessive and your curiosity omnivorous, if you grow up looking out at the sea and sense how vast the world is, if you seek excitement and explore the tiny gardens of beauty that lie within reach.

You need to do so while dreaming of the future and pursuing freedom, with that form of rebellion that is, in adolescence, the one way we come to know ourselves. Do all that and your utterly local being gives way to a universal feeling, which becomes your essence forever. Next thing you know you'll have put down those oh-so important roots just about everywhere.

If you grow up that way, at the water's edge, looking out at the sea day and night, you appreciate slowness and live with those images etched into your memory, from pebble beaches to steep mountains. What makes you local makes you original; you become who you've been all along. And if what you become is an architect, then those sensations turn into projects.

But you don't need to dwell on your roots, especially not before you turn sixty. There's other stuff to do before then. Nostalgia is dangerous. It can be permanently disabling. "Nostos" is another thing; the Greek word means returning home, not pining for the past. It is the sensation and recognition of your roots.

A5303

The sun had dipped halfway below the sea, and the sky was slate-colored, with flashes of deep purple in Sestri Ponente. It was impossible to distinguish the sky from the gray rooftops of the houses. The lighthouse was already lit and guiding ships through the dark with its bright beam. Our long, white, narrow ship was approaching the wharf, looking a little old-fashioned with its funnel located toward the bow and its aft deck empty. It made you think of discovery, science, and adventure. Rather than with cannons or rocket launchers, it bristled with antennae, dishes, and radars. Four officers in blue uniforms stared down at us from the bridge.

Initialed on its side were the letters A5303, the A standing for auxiliary. Meaning it was not a combatant ship, but designed to conduct oceanographic surveys, to study the mysteries of the deep and draw nautical charts. The only weapons on board are four muskets, just in case. "*Maniman*," they say in Genoa. You never know what tomorrow holds in store. Genoese prudence comes from its citizens' respect for the sea.

On the ship we were about to board, they had repaired the operating system and hull only a year before. They had also updated their equipment, so the ship had nothing to envy the most modern research vessels; it could survey depths of up to three thousand meters. At last, as the sailors lowered the boarding ramp, slowly uncoiling the rope, my father finally smiled.

✔ I say Atlantis exists, Carlo, and even if it doesn't, we should still look for it. Because it is a beautiful idea, the ideal destination no matter the journey. It must be out there.

The next morning, no later than eight, we would set sail and leave the city of water, the chalkboard city, behind. Where were we going? I still didn't know. It was better to sleep on it.

4.
THE ISLAND THAT WASN'T

Latitude 34°41'37" North, longitude 135°30'07" East. Now I know. We're headed to the Sea of Japan, where my father built the Kansai International Airport on an artificial island—the island that wasn't. I have spent the last twenty days in my cabin, practically quarantined. The ship was rolling heavily above deck, pounded by winds and sea spray. The one reprieve each day was the lunch shift and, on September 14, toasting the Explorer in honor of his birthday as we rounded the choppy waters of the Cape of Good Hope. Beyond that spit of rock, the Atlantic gave way to the Indian Ocean, though all oceans seem to belong to the same body of water. Especially when the crossing is long.

The weather was inclement, and so was the sea. I heard it howling and sloshing about. I saw it rough, flat, violent, stormy, frothing. Always, I fell into a daze.

I have neglected this diary until today, now that my nausea has abated. I had thought I wasn't susceptible to seasickness, that the time I had spent on sailboats would have made me immune. But I was wrong: traveling by water is unnatural for us terrestrials. Now the boatswain sharing my berth is making fun of me. He says that in Genoese the words *mare* (sea) and *male* (sick) both begin with M-Â. Anyone with intentions of setting sail ought to ponder that.

There are no mahogany desks or brass barometers in the cabins. That's just in the movies. There isn't even a porthole to look out. The roar of the engines muffles the noises outside, including the squawks of seagulls. Air from the vents keeps the temperature constant; you can't tell if the weather is hot or cold until you step back out on deck. But when there is *bulle-summe*, the waves knock over anything not tied down: bottles, eyeglasses, harmonicas, flashlights, and cellphones. The latter are the most dangerous object of them all.

Bullesumme is Genoese for rising tides, when the sea is neither rough nor calm. A little like a boiling pot. You have to grip the handrail as you walk. And if the waves rise after the sun has gone down, you can't even turn the lights on, as per warship regulations. After lowering the flag, the captain orders lights out and the lamps are turned off. The only lights left on are dim red spotlights that provide just enough light to see your feet. You have to hide from your enemies, even when there are none.

Giobatta

My berth is a steel cocoon, cut off from what is happening on the other side of the airtight door. There are two bunkbeds, and I sleep on the bottom bunk, which is less prone to rolling, the lateral motion of a ship. Top or bottom makes no difference when it comes to pitching, the up-down, seesawing motion. Above me sleeps Giobatta Molinari, the boatswain. Giobatta is short for Giovanni Battista. He is a robust man, suntanned though he doesn't seem the type, bald, of medium stature. His eyes, it goes without saying, are as blue as the sea. In the reddish fuzz of his left forearm nests a bluebird, a tattoo for sailors who have logged at least ten thousand miles.

Giobatta must be fifty, a venerable age for a sailor. He is also from Genoa, Prà to be precise, a district in the western part of the city famous for its brigantine shipyards and the basil grown around it. They say it's the best basil for making pesto.

The boatswain (*nostrommu* in Genoese) trusts no one and saves his breath for reprimanding the helmsmen when they're "pestling water in the mortar." Wasting time, in other words. Which is often, in his opinion. He launches into a long complaint about how the Navy isn't what it once was. How, once upon a time, the crew used to call the captain "*baccan*," or father. Only the captain knew the route, and the whole crew addressed him as "sir" and regarded him with reverence. *Sciü baccan*. Lord Father.

Everything, for Giobatta, used to be better. He misses the days of LPs, typewriters, Paolo Rossi's national soccer team; the days when people had the inner resources to amuse themselves; when nautical instruments—sextants, azimuth circles, and nocturnals—were more reliable.

Nauta pro nautis

We have not brought into port for a month and a half. Were the Suez Canal not closed, we would have cut across the Red Sea and shortened our journey.

Now we're just off the coast of Japan, after passing Sri Lanka with a light force two at our backs, entering the strait between Java and Sumatra, encountering the Island of Hainan and climbing back up to Taiwan. We'd be on our own in a salt desert were it not for the occasional fishing boat stockpiling tuna. Tuna fishing is more lucrative and respected here than anywhere else. At Tokyo's fish market, a giant bluefin tuna fetched a record-breaking seventy-four million yen.

I have yet to say much about this research vessel, the *Admiral Magnaghi*. Besides a destination—a minor detail—we have everything we need on board to map the ocean floor and uncover Atlantis: a multibeam echosounder, a sidescan sonar, a geodimeter, a marigraph, a bathythermograph, a box corer, a current meter, and various probes. I don't understand how they work, but Captain Ottavio Pasculli and the other officials and hydrographers know them inside out.

The name of the ship bodes well: Admiral Giovan Battista Magnaghi, another Giobatta, was a pioneer cartographer. He explored coasts, measured depths, directed the Naval Institute of Hydrography, and invented versions of such instruments as the "tilted" thermometer, the compass rose, and the reflecting circle. The ship's motto is "Nauta pro nautis". A sailor for sailors. The words are written on the crest of our ship currently scudding across the Sea of Japan.

My father knows these waters well. About thirty years ago he designed an airport in Osaka Bay. On an island that didn't exist. They made it out of nothing by cutting the summits of three or four hills to procure 200 million cubic meters of gravel and rock. There was not enough space for a runway on terra firma, and there was a law in effect that forbid airplanes from flying over the archipelago at night. But the law said nothing about the sea.

The Explorer scans the low, calm waves as they roll in and lap at the white prow.

It all began with a boat trip with Nori and Peter[2] one afternoon. I asked to visit the place, and the Japanese said it was pointless, that there was nothing but open sea, the island did not exist yet. What did this maniac want to see? they must have thought.

After I insisted, they agreed to take us. They must have been wondering what I was going out there to do. But they drove us

---

[2] Noriaki Okabe and Peter Rice worked on the Kansai project. Nori is a Japanese architect who collaborated with my father for twenty years. Peter (already mentioned) was an Irish engineer and cofounder of Atelier Piano & Rice. He passed away in 1992.

out into the middle of the bay anyway, because when it comes to courtesy no one rivals the Japanese.

The Dark

To cite just one example of their legendary courtesy: the Yakuza, the ancient and coldblooded Japanese mafia, once called a press conference to apologize to the inhabitants of Kobe for the noise disturbance caused by their gunfire. Everyone in Osaka Bay was extremely courteous too, my father recalls, as we pass by another fishing boat flying the Hinomaru, the flag with the red circle that, after the war and at the Americans' bidding, replaced the Kyokujitsuki, the flag depicting the rising sun with sixteen rays, which flapped in the wind on the fleet of the *Yamamoto*. The fishermen greeted us with a graceful bow.

We were at anchor, up on the deck taking notes, and I was making my usual sketches. The silence was only broken by our chaperones, who were suffering from seasickness; we'd been tossed about that day.

We were looking for clues, which any place can provide. Even the most absurd. No matter where you happen to be, there is always a little *genius loci* worth listening to, some precious indication that tells you how to proceed.

That day was no different. The sea is the underside of Earth, the side we know least. The slowness of the sea and a little silence is needed to grasp its reasons.

Bravery is born of that slowness. To brave the unknown, to probe the dark.

Marguerite Yourcenar also called on people to muster the courage, optimism, and a degree of determination to face the dark. She said we need to accept our fear of the unknown and never stop plumbing it.

To probe the dark is a beautiful metaphor, one that applies to the physical realm too. When you first enter a dark room, you can't see anything, but after a while, if you don't run away from fear, the eye adjusts. Your pupils dilate and you start to distinguish things. A profile, a shadow, a trace.

I ask myself, or rather I ask the Explorer, what he saw that time. Where did his idea come from? From being at sea? From the awesomeness of flying? From the land, which rattles and shakes like no other place on the planet?

April Fools'

My father and *baccan* Pasculli are consulting maps. When sailing along the coast we have to be careful of shoals just below the surface.

On that outing we were looking for direction, a stepping-stone to start us off. For an architect, freedom from the obligations of the real world is no great gift. It is far better to have clear direction and let context set the rules. Later, at the right moment, you might delight in breaking them. Like the staff on a large blank sheet of music.

Context is a boon, the material from which to draw, a score to interpret. Topography often supplies the necessary constraints. Total freedom is a myth; it paralyzes us. That day we were thinking more in terms of water and air than land.

Memories from my adolescence might have helped: the port where everything is constantly changing, the loads hanging from the cranes, the short-lived structures, the sailboat rigging.

I believe what we were thinking that afternoon can be seen in the flexible, lightweight form of the building. It was not a waste of time.

*

After the creation of the island, the maps had to be redrawn. Japan had grown fifteen square kilometers. Rumors also circulated that the island had sunk into the sea. On the front page of the *Asahi Shimbun*, or maybe the *Japan Times*, they said Kansai had gone under. Too bad the story appeared on April 1, 1990. But the Japanese, unaccustomed to pranks, believed it. It couldn't possibly sink, my father explained again and again. The story made him livid.

There are thousands of columns propping up the island. They extend down through twenty meters of water and another twenty of mud before finding anchor in solid rock. Each has a system of jacks on top that can be adjusted to achieve stability. In fact, the layer of mud did not settle evenly; in some spots it settled farther down, in others farther up. So the building could endure failures zone by zone. There were sensors that measured any up-down movements, and, when things exceeded the ten-millimeter tolerance level, adjustments were made.

Every pile foundation could be regulated with hydraulic jacks to correct the differential settlement—that's what I think it's called. Over the years, the 511-hectare-long, rectangular, man-made island has sunk an average of fifty centimeters, just as geologists had predicted.

Ship's Bells

In the bridge on the *Admiral Magnaghi*, two tolls alert people that it is mealtime. We eat in the wardroom with the ranking officers, as special guests. But there is no difference between the officers' menu and the crew's; the meal is the same.

People think ship's bells have been retired from modern ships, but in fact they continue to chime. Of course nowadays the bell is not the only thing that sets the pace of life on board. It is aided by a megaphone. Bells used to beat time on cargo ships, two tolls on the hour and one every half hour, and indicate shift changes. A rapid succession of tolls meant there was a fire; a cadenced chime, fog. Ship's bells have been largely replaced with whistles and horns, but they still summon people to eat.

Pietro Savasto, the chief cook on board, has prepared tagliolini with ground beef and niçoise olives. Niçoise olives have long accompanied Italian sailors, as has the oil made from them. We eat in silence, a good sign. All you can hear is the rumble of the engines propelling the nearly ninety-meter-long *Magnaghi* toward the coast of Honshu. The airport island sits a few miles offshore, where once there was nothing but a gulf of water and salt.

The building began to take shape while we were floating on the water. The idea for its thin shell structure came to us in the middle of the sea. Tracing signs in the air, Peter showed us how the structure would move in the event of a severe hurricane.

Our idea sprang from that reality, that unlimited source of inspiration. Hurricanes, and earthquakes too. Even floating, we had the sensation of latent seismic activity.

I couldn't wait. Ever since my early experiments, I had wanted to build such a structure, like an elastic skeleton that could absorb the forces of nature. Sooner or later you have to confront them. Nature is neither good nor evil. It is totally indifferent to the fragility of humankind. That is where the challenge arises.

At a certain point, Peter began talking about geometric shapes: hyperbolic paraboloids and, finally, toroids. He had a picture of a circular arc with a center thirteen kilometers below the earth that would trace the imaginary curve of the building on the surface.

Namazu

The telephone of the second in charge, ship lieutenant Elio Tamburini, is ringing. He's receiving notice of a possible earthquake. The danger alert system has a yellow catfish logo, because in ancient times they believed that cataclysms were caused by the enormous catfish, Namazu. Namazu lives underneath the archipelago and, every once and a while, flaps its tail. Fortunately, the god Kashima restrains it, but when Kashima loosens his grip, Namazu thrashes about, causing the ground and the sea to shake.

Not that we have reason to be particularly worried: on average there are a thousand earthquakes a year here, and the Japanese are prepared. We're floating on the surface of one of the most vulnerable countries in the world. There are nearly 150 volcanoes scattered across the islands, the majority of them active. Not counting those on the seabed yet to be accounted for.

We are sailing over two overlapping shelves of Earth's crust. One tectonic plate is pulling north, while the other is pushing in the opposite direction, and in the middle lies a rift of magma. So, when there is a quake under the water, the coasts are assailed by gigantic tsunami waves. As if that weren't enough, there is also the unknown variable of typhoons, though Osaka Bay is relatively shielded from them. It is hard to find a country more prone to natural disasters.

We are high up on the bridge, between the mizzen mast and the funnel, trailing a wake of white foam. We are traveling at a speed of twelve knots, maybe a little less. The Constructor lived through his share of earthquakes on the job. In thirty-eight months, thirty-six were recorded, all higher than five on the Richter scale. That included the devastating earthquake that destroyed Kobe after construction had been completed. For forty-five seconds—an eternity—

the vault of the airport swayed fifty centimeters in either direction.

They notified me at my studio in Paris. It was January 17, 1995. It was bitter cold, as I remember.

A magnitude-seven quake, of tremendous force. The ground shifted eighteen centimeters horizontally and twelve vertically. The Kansai Airport was the exact same distance from the epicenter as Kobe, which was destroyed, yet this building, to all appearances flimsy and lightweight, came out unscathed.

So you see why the notion of building light is not simply a question of form. It originates from the need to survive natural disasters, a need that is then sublimated into form.

Earthquakes move in one of two ways: vertical or horizontal ground motion. If a building is cumbersome, once it begins to move, holding it still becomes difficult. The weight is important because earthquakes exert enormous telluric force. The lighter a building, the less force is needed to hold it still.

Lightness and flexibility are fundamental because they absorb the energy of the impact and keep the building from splitting apart. Naturally, a building should not move in sync with the seismic motion, otherwise it becomes an unstoppable seesaw.

The toroidal structure that Peter began to develop promised a stable shape where seismic stress was perfectly distributed.

Wherever you look in Japan, things are built lightly as a matter of self-defense. Japanese children are taught to fear four things: earthquakes, thunder, fires, and fathers. In that order. In major department stores, day-after sections carry everything you need to survive. And a volcano, Mount Fuji, with its perfect conical form and snowy peak towering above the *sakura* blossoms, is the symbol not only of the country but of Shintoism and the identity of its people.

The Intelligence of Oil

Yet the earthquake in Kobe overwhelmed even those accustomed to aftershocks. The airport remained the one means of connection between the impact zone and the rest of the world. The elevated highway collapsed on its side, and buildings fell like dominoes. Entire neighborhoods of wood houses overlooking the sea burned down. The Japanese learned from that experience; now gas tanks automatically switch off. They defend themselves against nature with the gift that nature gave us: intelligence.

Maybe if we were really an intelligent species, my father and I would not have come looking for Atlantis. He had even confided his secret wish to the captain. Can it exist? Perhaps no one knows.

But I could not help thinking that Plato, philosopher that he was, sank the island to warn us about the transient nature of fortune. There may be a point to this periplus, but it has thus far escaped me. Maybe it doesn't matter whether Atlantis is real or imagined. Maybe we just need to move, to set out on a journey, to ask questions.

Now and again the lieutenant's cell phone buzzes with updates about the intensity of the earthquake, which appears to be slight. On top of that, the next morning a tropical depression is supposed to plow into Hokkaido, the northernmost Japanese island farthest from our position. In the United States hurricanes are given a name, while in Japan each hurricane is numbered in chronological order based on when it appeared that year. Japan's system reflects the precision of its meticulous and resolute people. When, during the opening ceremony of the Kansai construction site, the Surveyor asked when work on the airport would be completed, he was told the exact date three years later. He jokingly asked what time of day it would be completed. The Japanese conferred. "Noon," they answered. And so it was.

Sailors love to tell stories about tornadoes and tempests. One night, Giobatta kept me up until two in the morning explaining to me how all it took to calm rough waves was a few drops of oil, a fact I did not know. Logbooks attest to galleons, on the brink of shipwreck, pouring barrels of oil overboard. And in *Naturalis Historia*, Pliny the Elder mentions the miraculous ability of oil to mitigate storms, without dragging in religion or the supernatural.

It was science. Oil calms rough waves. All kinds of animal and vegetable oils can do the trick. The best is olive oil, because it spreads rapidly. But olive oil has the disadvantage of congealing at two degrees centigrade. Therefore, it is best to mix olive oil with oils less susceptible to the cold. Among animal oils, seal and whale are excellent, and among vegetable oils, cotton, flax, and turpentine.

Canvas sacks are filled with oil-soaked rags, poked with holes, and dropped into the sea. They use about three liters of oil an hour. The Explorer was familiar with the technique, though I don't believe he had ever been put in a position to test it.

Sea storms produce waves on the surface of the water that, pushed by the wind, grow progressively taller. On the back of the waves there forms an increasingly large layer of rippling water that is driven forward.

On the other hand, the face of a wave, the side falling forward, remains sheltered and tends to become steeper and steeper. That is how breakers are created, and breakers pummel the sterns of fleeing ships. If the wind continues to pick up, the situation can become dangerous. The crest of the wave falls forward and breaks on the hull.

That's when pouring oil on a rough sea has the almost magic effect of increasing surface tension and creating a film that prevents the wind from getting traction on the water. Oil changes the waves into a heavy swell, so that they do not break in that area.

Intelligence is needed to govern water. My father sees the power of a drop of oil as a metaphor. A single building, he says, can revitalize an entire neighborhood. Similarly, in *Invisible Cities*, Italo Calvino writes that even in a city that suffers there is always a happy corner, something that works right, and you have to cling to that. According to Calvino, fragments of happy cities are constantly developing and disappearing, hidden in unhappy cities. From a droplet or a fragment, you can start over again.

The idea of droplets is beautiful, because it speaks to the strength of the little guy. Like the story of David and Goliath.

The same idea is at the heart of the work I do at my G124[3] office in the Italian senate, investing in urban peripheries and revitalizing them. The neglected, denigrated suburban areas of cities are often treated as emotional wastelands. We'll talk more about that later.

By making, in part, local interventions—droplets again—you set in motion a virtuous circle of regeneration. Building places for people, where people who share the same values can get together and partake in the rituals of a city. Schools, theaters, libraries—all meeting places are droplets.

That is what Calvino means by the fragments of cities, and it is with fragments that we must make a start.

Construction-site Pride

There was a lot of traffic in the bay back when the airport was being built. Security vessels, barges loaded with rock,

[3] See Chapter 11.

ferries carrying laborers to work or home. The adventure of the Kansai construction site lasted over three years and enlisted six and sometimes as many as ten thousand workers, all scattered around the island. Discipline was the watchword.

On more than one occasion I had to make a brief address to the construction workers on the island, in the morning, before work began. Thousands of people would be listening, all of them stretching and warming up. They had on yellow helmets, harnesses, water bottles strapped to their shoulders, and carabiners. They looked like an army of samurai.

They would warm up to music, as if for a sporting event. They appeared to be barefoot, but they were actually wearing traditional Japanese shoes, the kind with the big toe separated from the other toes. The carpenters preferred them to boots, because the shoes made it easier to balance on the girders.

Such moments take me back to my father's small construction site. You see yourself as a kid again, observing everything, sitting on a pile of sand. I always loved going to the site with my father and watching something grow from nothing.

For a kid, a construction site is a place of wonder: one day all you see is sand and loose bricks, the next thing you know, there's a freestanding wall, and eventually the whole thing turns into a tall, solid building for people to live.

It transforms into something that defies the force of gravity. I believe that in my subconscious there is a direct correlation, which has never been broken, between those piles of sand and my construction sites today.

My father always told me, if you want to make something well, you need to pay careful attention and devote enough hours to it. I still believe that.

A storm is brewing, and I am not talking about bad weather.

I'm not sure what has happened, but our boatswain is scream-
ing at the helmsmen. They hadn't followed his orders quickly
enough, orders that he imparts by blowing on a copper whistle
attached to a chain around his neck. The duration and quality
of the whistle blows correspond to various commands, from
weighing anchor to cleaning the latrines. The whistle is also
used to salute NCOs passing down the gangway port. Where
did my father go? He's gotten lost in the past.

I think about my father often.

It was right after the war, in 1945. Even then he seemed old
to me, though he was only fifty. He was your typical Genoese,
reserved and taciturn. Perhaps more foreman than entrepre-
neur. But at the construction site he always wore a hat and
blazer, sometimes a tie. His elegance aside, the point is, he was
always there, working alongside everyone else.

I was a scrawny kid, and my mother, your grandmother Rosa,
liked to take me to the countryside in Ovada for the summer. It
was an obsession of hers, as was her desire to make me study
and read any and everything. She was the tenacious guardian of
an undisciplined son and the school dunce.

But I preferred the city to the country and liked playing at my
father's construction site. After dinner, he would bring his workers
over to the house. One of them was a small, stocky, muscular guy
named Moro. Another was Carletto della Rocca Grimalda, who
never stood still. And then there was Luigi, the trusted watchman.

Together they would go over what they'd done that day and
what they had to do the following day. My father would dictate
and I would slowly copy out the day's report on the slate board
in the kitchen. MANHOURS: 8. TOTAL TO DATE: 72. RC'D 4
TRUCKLOADS OF SAND FROM THE PO. PURCHASED 12
DOZEN 100 MM NAILS. I think those evenings helped spark my
passion for building.

He still hadn't explained what he would say during his addresses to the army of samurai. Some people claim that the Japanese have a work ethic that has been lost in the rest of the world. Carpenters are not the only ones who practice a morning ritual. Everyone wears a uniform: students (who dress in Prussian-style attire), plumbers, taxi drivers, intellectuals, gangsters covered in tattoos, even undertakers and *sararīman*, i.e., white-collar workers. Sociologists say that in Japan conformity is the most coveted virtue, whereas being excluded from a group is the worst form of humiliation. ✓

The atmosphere on board subsided. To demonstrate his disapproval, Giobatta had locked himself in his cabin after inveighing against his underlings, calling them good-for-nothings and so on.

What did I say during those speeches? I said what I had already said at the groundbreaking ceremony. I gave the same address that all architects have to make in Japan, where there is a ritual for everything.

I had to warn the workers not to take any pointless risks, since, though the architect decides how a project is to be carried out, he himself doesn't perform the job. He delegates the construction of it to others.

I would say, more or less, this: "Friends, we architects came up with this building while we were sitting around a table. It is up to you to build it while hanging in the air. Take care not to get hurt. I appreciate the risks you take and thank you for making our dream a reality. Do it safely. I am giving you our plans but use caution and look after your own safety first."

That's what I would say to the workers.

But my address was not the end of the safety ritual, which has a civic and political component. Of six thousand laborers, five hundred were in charge of keeping the site clean, safe, and orderly. There was something theatrical about it: the carpenters are light on their feet, like acrobats. Every move was performed with great precision.

In the evening the team would clean up the site, securing the machines and steel beams and all the stored materials to weather any aftershocks during the night. The next morning, they would start all over again. Those of us in the office took great satisfaction in the fact that nobody ever got hurt on that site.

I like, and have always liked, this display of affection for those who do the job.

When I was a young architect, I conducted experiments too. Thanks to my brother Ermanno, who was ten years older than me and took over my father's business. He was proud of me and always encouraging.

One day, in 1965 I think, we were mounting a lightweight structure that was suspended from a crane. There were three of us, plus the crane operator. It was an unsafe operation, since it is never prudent to be standing under a load dangling from a crane.

Carmelo and Moro were bolting down the base of the structure, while I stood at a distance and kept my eye on the vertical upright. I instinctively felt a little ashamed, so I went and stood by them until they'd finished the job.

It was hardly a great act of courage, but I never did like the division between designer and builder, between saying and doing.

I remember once there was a tensile structure where the cables were stretched so taut that they could have snapped. I knew it was dangerous to be there, but building involves participating in an adventure together, using your intelligence to deal with risks, bridging gaps.

Constructing buildings fills people with pride and brings them together. A job well done is a gesture of civic responsibility and a gesture toward peace.

The Enigma of Yonaguni

Our approach to the coast of Honshu is proceeding briskly. We can glimpse its profile on the horizon, still blurry and shrouded in mist. The Explorer has borrowed the commander's twelve by fifty binoculars, but I doubt he can see anything. It's as if we've been dropped into a glass of water and anise.

We reach Kansai, where my father had, in a way, created an Atlantis, an upside-down Atlantis that, instead of sinking to the ocean floor, was lifted out of the water by human hands. I'm not sure if afterward we'll be setting a course for Yonaguni, the island farthest west. Yonaguni became famous at the end of the last century when a group of scuba divers discovered a pyramid-like structure not unlike the Egyptian pyramids. Though it could be a natural formation. Since then, despite the danger of hammerhead sharks, many divers have devoted themselves to studying it. Some claim it is the legendary lost continent Mu. Others Atlantis.

Thanks to the equipment on board the *Magnaghi*, we have a chance to unveil the mystery. The equipment can probe depths that the sun can't reach. At a depth of thirty meters, only blue and green manage to penetrate. At depths of fifty to two hundred meters, they too disappear, and it is total darkness. Sailors used to imagine that these aphotic territories were home to the monsters that adorn ancient maps: fish with razor-sharp teeth, snakes with lions' manes, killer octopuses.

That same ancestral fear cast a shadow over the Kansai project. In fact, during the initial stages, they had considered building a buoyant island unattached to the ocean floor. A debate raged over the consequences of casting a shadow over such a large area of warm water, which had no precedent in nature. All they had to compare it to was the sea under the arctic shelf, except there the water hovers around freezing temperature. Biologists worried that unknown lifeforms might proliferate and wondered aloud what monsters might arise as a result. That was one of the reasons the idea was abandoned.

But I don't think my father is interested in Yonaguni; it isn't his Atlantis. He had sought Atlantis on this island of airplanes, where at last, after forty days at sea, we dock. I look around while he sizes up his creature, as if it were his prodigal son. For an airport that sorts through eighteen million passengers a year, Kansai is in good shape, a tribute to travel, adventure, the drive to discover. There is a sense of expectation, as if something were always about to happen.

The airplanes, with their colorful tails, own the island. They are the gods that Kansai worships. One with a blue and gold tail is taking off for Hanoi; in ten minutes another will land from Helsinki. Passengers stream this way and that, happy to be leaving, happy to be coming back. There is something strangely touching about arrivals and departures.

My father hands me a sheet of paper. It is an email from a traveler named Paul dated November 30, 2016. Subject: A thank you to Mr. Piano.[4]

Dear Mr. Piano,

I did not know it was one of your buildings but it inspired me as a humble and weary traveler to write this:

I have found an airport I don't want to leave! It's normally a case of "get me outta here," but Kansai International is so beautiful I want to stay. It is in such stark contrast to all other airports I have ever visited. It is so simple and elegant with a central terminal building the size of a cathedral, all

---

[4] The authors thank Paul for his letter. To protect his privacy, his last name has been omitted.

shimmering glass and steel that rolls over you like a huge wave. This being Japan, all is harmonious, restrained and perfectly functional as well as being full of calming beauty. It is huge yet so quiet and relaxing. Night has fallen and it is wonderfully lit. Two wings stretch out from the main building, extending like huge tunnels down which travelers are transported on their way to planes that sit neatly side by side. Everything is effortless. It is the perfect marriage of form and function. It compares with any of the temples and gardens I have just visited . . . Thank you.

Nice, says the Constructor. But he isn't satisfied. He keeps scanning the area, dogged by some error or regret, something he might have done better. A flaw that, in a soft voice, he is on the verge of admitting.

Hmph. Not enough light in this space.
We should have let more through from the ceiling.
Don't you see how dark it is?

In the meantime, Second Lieutenant Egidio Valente read the forecast aloud. Overcast with light showers, wind from the west at eight to ten knots. Wind force two with local winds from the southeast. After stocking up on supplies—provisions for the pantry, fuel for the tanks—we set sail again.

Never trust weather forecasts, says the boatswain. Yet it is a practice that sailors relish, especially by observing the color of the sky and the shape of the clouds. On a ship, conversations about the weather never end. Are the clouds lenticular? Cirrus? Cumulus? Incus? Cirrocumulus? The weather gives rise to heated arguments. Even the occasional punch is thrown.

5.

RETRACING CAPTAIN COOK'S ROUTE

ay seventy-seven of the periplus undertaken by Carlo (the present author) and his father Renzo. Night has fallen and the water, pitch-black at these latitudes, blurs with the sky. It is mid November and twenty-seven degrees centigrade. Cyclone season begins in December. Soon we will be in sight of the Amédée Lighthouse, which signals the Boulari Passage, the one navigable entrance to the Port of Nouméa. All around us, hidden beneath the shallow waters, is barrier reef.

Our charts provide detailed descriptions of lighthouses: how tall they are, how often they flash, from what distance they can be seen. Atop an isle of white sand, our lighthouse is over fifty meters tall, and its light can be seen from twenty-five miles away. The Amédée Lighthouse is made of cast iron, prebuilt in France and later transported, in parts, to New Caledonia.

Once we are portside of Amédée, we have another two hours before reaching our destination, latitude 22°16'34" South, longitude 166°27'25" East. We have more or less followed the route that Captain James Cook took when he discovered these islands at the end of the 1700s. Cook sailed in a sloop called *Resolution*, and the spectacle that opened up before his eyes could not have been much different from the view today: a coast of tall, straight trees thrust into the air.

In the dark they almost look like moored sailboats. But they are Cook pines, or *Araucaria columnaris*, rimming the shores of an archipelago that the British explorer christened New

Caledonia, because they reminded him of the Scottish Highlands. When he disembarked, Cook took with him an entourage of naturalists, philosophers, cartographers, astronomers, and adventurers. The Melanesian Kanaks he encountered called him *tea*, or chief, the highest of honors. In return he left them a couple of pigs and one of his dogs. They had never seen a dog before.

On this island my father built the Kanak cultural center named after Jean-Marie Tjibaou, the separatist leader who was assassinated in the 1980s. Something about the project doesn't quite satisfy him. But, as we sip coffee in the wardroom with Corvette Captain Pasculli, now isn't the time to mention it.

On the walls hangs a shiny copperplate matrix of an ancient nautical map of Pantelleria, a 1:100,000 scale map meticulous both for the accuracy of its handmade drawings and for the work that went into its creation. The map shows the characteristics of the ocean floor, landmarks, depths that had been discovered by lowering a rope with a weight tied to the end. There are special devices on board the *Magnaghi*, like echo sounders and sonar, comprised of a projector and transducer. Duccio Frascaro, the second lieutenant from Livorno and head of the hydrography division, told me how they worked. The projector sends a series of waves, which bounce off the sea bottom and are then reflected back toward the transducer. By calculating the time it takes for the waves to reach the bottom and come back up, and the speed with which the waves travel underwater, you can establish the distance between the bottom and the keel of the ship.

There is another strange instrument guarded in the belly of the ship, kept apart from the other equipment so that ferromagnetic materials do not create interference. The job of this hidden compass is to supply, without fail, the radar and autopilot with its heading relative to true north. The Surveyor claims we all have a hidden compass that tells us which way to go, that prevents us from drifting off course. Whether we listen to our hidden compass or not is another matter.

HMS Resolution

It is Sunday, and the cook, who is also the commissary insofar as he manages the care of the pantry, has prepared baked lasagna, his specialty. The wine is better too, a ruby-colored Nebbiolo from the Langhe region in Piedmont.

The Explorer has set the 1781 edition of *The Voyages of Captain James Cook* down on the table. He must have had it with him since his work on the Tina Peninsula, where birds of prey circle the lagoon, parrots chirp, mangrove crabs snap their claws, and, more importantly, the Kanaks believe that the winds rustling in the pine trees are the whispers of their ancestors.

My father keeps talking about how the pine island caught Cook's attention for reasons that were far from poetic. Cook thought the pines would be perfect for rebuilding the rigging of his sloop. On his long voyages, he was always losing bowsprits and spars, so he brought the pine trunks on board for spare parts. With their thin branches that, once chopped down and hewn with an ax, had no knots, the pines seemed made for the job. The Explorer hands me the book, full of flags marking the pages he has taken an interest in.

As I leaf through *The Voyages*, the boatswain, curious, comes over. He, too, considers the captain, who was killed in Hawaii while tirelessly searching for new lands to name, a legend. Today there is Mount Cook, the Cook Islands, Cook Strait, Cook's Bay, the Cook Ice Cap, and, on the northeast coast of Australia, Cooktown.

Cook's diary relates the departure from Sheerness, on June 21, 1772, of the *Resolution*, or HMS *Resolution*, 111 feet long and 35 feet wide. It also details the provisions on board: twenty-seven tons of hardtack, 7,637 pieces of salted beef and 14,200 pieces of pork, 850 kilos of suet, 1,400 of raisins, 1,100 liters of oatmeal, 800 of olive oil and 900 kilos of sugar. Supplies to combat scurvy included 2,400 liters of malt, nine tons of sauerkraut, 1,800 kilos of salted cabbage, 180 of mustard, and 113 liters of carrot marmalade. As for alcohol, they brought on board nineteen tons of beer and 2,400 liters of wine.

Giobatta is enthralled but has to run off, because it is almost time to dock. He is responsible for supervising the helmsmen on the deck as they check to ensure the lines don't unravel, the winches are sufficiently greased, and the chains don't get twisted in the anchor locker. In the Italian navy a boatswain is not a rank but a job performed by the eldest and most experienced helmsman. His rank is first marshal sub-lieutenant, and he is a fount of traditional sailing wisdom. Few people can judge the sturdiness of bitts, few know the secrets of knots or how much an anchor weighs. Giobatta is one of them.

My father wants his book back. He almost tears it out of my hands while I am mid-sentence: "By twice visiting the tropical sea, I had not only settled the situation of some old discoveries, but made many new ones, and left, I conceive, very little more to be done even in that part."[5] You can't accuse Cook of modesty.

I'm left wondering if anything remains to be discovered on this little planet. If Atlantis really existed. If Aristotle, Plato's student, was right when he memorably dismissed the mystery: "The man who dreamed it up also made it vanish."

---

[5] James Cook, *The Voyages of Captain James Cook*, edited by Nicholas Thomas (Zenith Press, 2016)

A Trunk on the Tina Peninsula

I also wonder what the Explorer was looking for when he entered the competition to build a cultural center on the opposite end of the planet. Maybe, in a world where everything has already been uncovered, architecture is one of the few enduring adventures into the unknown. The bright strobes of the Amédée guide us toward Grande Terre, the principal island. I don't feel like talking tonight, I prefer to stargaze in silence and be alone with my thoughts. But a boat isn't big enough to keep your distance.

It has become tradition, almost. I never design a project without first visiting the site. As a kind of moral principle. If I don't attempt to learn about the place by entering into dialogue with it, listening to it, conversing with it, walking it, exploring its terrain; put simply, if I don't follow these rituals, I can't get started.

When Milly and I had just gotten married, we traveled to Osaka, to the site of Kansai, and from there went on to Nouméa. We stayed a few days, traveling up and down the island, constantly making little sketches, taking notes. She followed me out of curiosity. Or maybe she was just being patient.

I sat for a long time on a tree trunk. Many trunks were strewn about the ground, owing to all the trees that get knocked over during hurricane season. Fortunately we were there at the time of the trade winds, and the weather was nice. A short distance from Nouméa, the land around the Tina Peninsula is fertile.

I couldn't talk to the client, because direct contact is forbidden in a competition. I was sitting on the trunk and letting my thoughts run freely. Places speak, it's true. This one in particular. The trade winds on these islands have a very special sound.

I could hear two of them clearest: the lively chop of the open sea and the silent, still waters of the lagoon in the interior. The place had a dual nature, and that is where the idea for an asymmetrical building came from, with the side facing the sea different from the side facing the lagoon, a building that would create a natural ventilation system by harnessing the continuous breeze of the trade winds.

It all came to me while I sat there, silently, on a tree trunk. That's why I believe that places speak, that they have a language.

There was a sense of travel and adventure in the air, and the ghost of Cook hovering about.

Morpheus is approaching, since sailing facilitates sleep. It must be the exhaustion of keeping your balance, of constantly climbing up and down stairs, of being rocked by the sea. Apparently, when we sway up and down, the cerebellum sends a weak signal to your nerves and slows your heart rate. I don't know if that's true, but staying awake on board is hard, at least for me.

Not for my father and not tonight. Maybe it's my fault, asking him all these questions. Why New Caledonia? How did he arrive at this idea? But he is partially to blame for withholding his answers so long, sometimes days.

See, if you want ideas you just need to decide to have them. You need to be brave and you need to take risks without being afraid to make mistakes. Everyone should act like this, especially young people: seize the moment and then throw yourself into your work.

Don't take my word for it. Octavio Paz used to say that poetry is the "*hija del azar; fruto del cálculo.*" The daughter of chance, the fruit of calculation. Of tireless activity. Creative works may be born of intuition but they are the fruit of thought.

An idea before it has become an idea is nothing, less than a flash.

An idea arises, and you can't tell whether you've heard it, said it or done it before. There is almost always the echo of someone close to you, someone with whom you work. You look around, you try to remember, nothing comes to mind.

When it first materializes, an idea is a ghost. It doesn't come into focus. In fact you often regard it with suspicion. Then it returns and you muster the courage to give it a form—spoken, written or drawn. You make a sketch—quickly and roughly—so that it doesn't become a trap.

Coming up with ideas isn't hard, but you have to throw yourself into them, and you often risk making errors.

Beware of easy fantasies. They're a trap.

Yes, I was sitting on a tree trunk looking around.

But I was looking with the eyes of someone with forty years of experience.

Islomania

The building was to be a cultural center for the Kanak people. I don't believe he knew much about the three hundred tribes or their twenty-nine different languages, nor about how they live in harmony with nature. A minor detail in his book. If he isn't familiar with a subject, he turns to someone who is. That was how the French anthropologist Alban Bensa got involved. Bensa had lived with the Kanaks for a long time and written essays about them, including 'Nouvelle-Calédonie: un paradis dans la tourmente.' The subtitle speaks volumes about the turbulence of Cook's archipelago, and I am not just referring to hurricanes.

The very idea of a cultural center dedicated to Jean-Marie Tjibaou, the separatist leader who was later assassinated, was a gesture by the French to make amends for colonialism. Tyranny and broken promises had also given rise to legends, like the legend of the Cargo, the ship that came down from heaven to lavish the archipelago with food and wealth. There actually was a ship, called the *Rhin*, which was supposed to provide the Kanak with supplies after they had been devastated by famine. Instead what came ashore were French soldiers, missionaries hoping to convert the Kanaks, and guard dogs. On the Isle of Pines they also opened a penal colony to which three thousand political dissidents of the Paris Commune were deported. While they were at it, the French also exported counterfeiters, conmen, and murderers, figuring that down there they wouldn't bother anybody.

Islands-cum-prisons are a trusted expedient. My father's colleague Daedalus built a labyrinth on Crete to house the minotaur. The Romans relegated their enemies to Mljet, an island in the southern Adriatic, because it was so full of snakes that there was no need to post guards. Napoleon Bonaparte was first imprisoned on Elba and later St. Helena, where the English had also sent the Zulu king Cetshwayo into exile.

Descendants of colonists, known as *caldoches*, still live in New Caledonia. They make up a third of the population. The Paris government devised a plan to grow the community, which was full of men and no women: they sent a cargo ship full of orphan girls.

But not all of the stories about New Caledonia involve exploitation and deportation. The islands are also blessed, and one can lead a carefree and happy life there. Many utopias have been born that have never failed to infect those of us in the west, lured by the freeing thought of escaping to lost paradises. The term "islomania" was coined to describe this affliction, a syndrome that manifests in an inability to resist land surrounded by water.

A few years ago, in La Digue, in the Seychelles, I met an Italian from Cuneo who had married a native. He lived in a cheerful house surrounded by palm and banana trees, a short walk from a sandy beach. But he wasn't happy.

He missed the mountain mists, how they make everything

wonderfully indefinite. He had a friend from Paris who had also relocated to the island with his wife. His friend kept a yellow metro card in his wallet, never went anywhere without it. He lived in an even bigger cottage with an even lusher yard. Yet not even dawn at the equator, when things regain their color, seemed to move him.

The Ise Grand Shrine

Michelangelo Antonioni wanted to set a film in the Tjibaou Cultural Center. Tonino Guerra had already written the script, about a woman who leaves London and finds herself in a different world that changes her life. Sophia Loren was slated to play the lead. But nothing came of it, because it was difficult for Antonioni to travel, though he continued to work and dream.

Escape is not, however, always dictated by the illusion of burying one's past. Sometimes all it takes is to stray from the beaten path. The Fortunate Isles, which would appear to be the Canary Islands, were so called because they were only encountered by chance or good luck, while trying to escape a storm or being driven by the currents. In fact, when sailors tried to return to the islands, they couldn't find them anymore.

To track them down again they would have needed coordinates, but at the time people navigated by the stars and could establish only their latitude, not their longitude. The one way to find the meridian was to compare the local time with the time of departure. But back then watches were not accurate enough, even less so when tossed about by the ocean. Cook was the first person to solve the problem by using a marine chronometer on his travels in this archipelago. Ever since, we have been able to calculate the exact location of every place on the planet.

Traveling is like exploring, understanding. To travel is to discover.

Read Cavafy. He wrote marvelous poems. What matters is not reaching Ithaca but making the journey to find Ithaca. Sure, you need a destination, whatever it takes, even if you know you might never reach it.

Cavafy may be writing metaphorically, yet it's true that every trip holds surprises, that looking for one thing, you find another. It is a little like searching for a book in a vast library: we know we might never find the book we came for, but we will find many other books that may turn out to be even more meaningful to us.

For Italians, and Europeans in general, another important aspect about traveling is that we realize how lucky we are to have been born where we were.

Clearly my father is not drawn to getting away from the world. He prefers the civilized beauty of our homeland to the wilds, which are too easily grown accustomed to. Unlike the wild, the built environment can be perfected: humans have always been eager to subdue nature by building roads, dams, levees, and bridges, and by cultivating fields. Like Prometheus giving humanity the gift of fire for the progress of civilization.

In my opinion, what intrigued him was diversity, the fact that the whole Pacific is the cradle of a particular culture. As is Japan, where a building does not endure by being conserved for millennia, but by being rebuilt time and time again. The repeated act, not the stone, makes things eternal.

A long time ago we visited the Ise Shrine, a place of Shinto worship. Every twenty years the main temple is demolished and rebuilt, a practice that began in the seventh century and continues to this day. It was last rebuilt in 2013 and will be built again in 2033. The cycle is also a metaphor for life: at twenty, the youth come to Ise to learn how to build the temple; at forty they rebuild it; and when they turn sixty, they teach the next generation that will take their place. The Constructor was with me that day in the Ise-Shima National Park on Honshu.

The idea of rebuilding the same temple every twenty years might seem strange. In fact, there is a streak of madness in it, but there is also profound wisdom.

V In Ise, when they cut down a tree, they mark the north-facing side of the trunk, so that it will continue to face north when it is used in construction. Then the trunks are kept in water for five years, and for another five they are left to dry in a well-ventilated area. That speaks volumes about Japanese and Asian Pacific culture, where emphasis is placed on the repetition of an act rather than on the durability of an artifact. A tradition passed down from generation to generation.

The same happens in New Caledonia, where I had to think Kanak. I used to kid Marie-Claude Tjibaou, Jean-Maie's widow, that I was becoming more Kanak than her.

They are a bit like those of us from the Mediterranean: we both respect our elders, revere our ancestors, show gratitude toward nature, and latch onto our roots. Every village in that vast part of the world has a *chefferie*, a council of elders that decides the most important issues of the tribe.

I too was raised in a culture that recognizes the dignity and wisdom of its elders. But the Kanak practice more explicit rituals and are less reserved about externalizing their feelings. They have a ceremony for everything here.

Iceberg

The Explorer likes to use the iceberg as a metaphor (fortunately, in these seas, we're in no danger of running into one). He loves figures of speech: weighed anchors, loose cannons, kaleidoscopes, sails, arcs, shelters, and mending. Some people accuse him of avoiding specialistic jargon to cast spells, that it is all a ploy to persuade others. Personally, I think he uses these phrases to make himself understood.

Whatever the case may be, in his opinion, architecture is like an iceberg: Only the tip is visible. The rest sits beneath the surface. The forces that remain hidden—society, history, geography, the environment, music, science, movies, math, art, ecology, and anthropology—sustain architecture. It is kept afloat by these other disciplines and reflects them all. Inevitably, he says.

All of these things must be contended with every day. It adds complexity and adventure to the life of an architect.

At nine A.M. you are a pragmatic constructor, an avid world explorer. At eleven you turn into a designer, drawn to the complexities of cities and the fragility of Earth. At three P.M., a humanist, curious about everything: art, music, people, communities.

The next day you begin all over again.

The way you see things changes as your gaze constantly flits from one branch to another. It's like pinball, bouncing between invention, civic anxiety, and the quest for beauty, elusive beauty.

In New Caledonia each island preserves its own history. The people of New Caledonia do not speak dialects with a common root but genuinely distinct languages. In fact, because they were from different tribes, Jean-Marie Tjibaou and his wife Marie-Claude had to communicate in French to understand one another. Marie-Claude speaks Paicî, the language of the eastern and western coast; but forty miles away, in Hienghène, her husband's village, another language is spoken. The northern languages are Nyelâyu, Kumak, Caac, Yuanga, Jawe, Nemi, Fwâi, Pije, Pwaamei, and Pwapwâ. The central are Cèmuhî, Paicî, Ajië, Arhâ, Arhö, Orowe, Neku, Zire, Tîrî,

Xârâcùù, and Xârâgùrè. In the south, they speak Ndrumbea and Numèè. The three languages of the Loyalty Islands facing the eastern coast of Grande Terre are Drehu, Iaai, and Nengone. Lastly, there is Fagauvea, the one New Caledonian language that belongs to the Polynesian family, which is spoken in northern Ouvéa. The cultural center had to convey that complexity, or at least attempt to.

So my father could not help but seek assistance from anthropology.

Of course, architecture is all about crossover. That has often been the case, and this was the greatest adventure of them all.

With the composers Berio, Boulez, Abbado, Pollini, and Accardo, my work has overlapped with music. It has also overlapped with art, film, literature, science. With several other travel companions. Creating spaces for all sorts of people and fields is the fate of the architect. There is nothing more vital than working on a project with people from other disciplines, because you experience the hopes and disappointments and joys of discovery together.

But you do not speak the same language. Every discipline has its own language and you have to avoid falling into the trap of confusing one for the other. An architect is an explorer, he lives on the frontier and, every so often, goes out to see what is lying on the other side. Living on the frontier means evading borders.

Hurricanes and Typhoons

Dead calm. Now the air, which earlier had carried an earthy smell, is still and odorless. I hear the captain on the bridge conferring with Tamburini, his second in command, and Lieutenant Valente. They are checking the aneroid barometer and pointing at low-lying clouds hugging the water

in the distance. The helmsman, Paolo Giannutri, the petty officer first class who was serving on the frigate *Zeffiro*, tells me
that the calm before the storm is not just a figure of speech.

When a storm develops, warm, moist air builds in the atmosphere and is driven upward to the highest clouds of the oncom-
ing storm. Hence the momentary calm. I hope that isn't the
case. In any event, our bow is pointed straight at the port.
Besides, as Giobatta never tires of repeating, a real sailor shows
what he is made of in a storm.

There were tons of typhoons during the construction on
Noumèa. The islands in the Southern Hemisphere are battered by raging winds, cyclones, and tropical storms. At least
two or three times a year, especially between December and
April.

In twenty-six months of work we had three hurricanes with
winds gusting at 250 kilometers an hour. We watched them with
our hearts in our throats.

But, by flexing, the building withstood them.

I have always been drawn to the idea of designing in the
Pacific for the chance to contend with a culture founded on lightness, with the idea that strength lies in flexibility. In Japan flexibility matters because of earthquakes; in New Caledonia, because
of violent hurricanes.

Eliminating mass from a structure teaches you how to make
the form work. And to look for its poetry. While seeking lightness
you find something else that is precious: transparency. By eliminating mass you also eliminate the opaqueness of the material.
Eliminating mass is an art, which I began to develop a long time
ago, watching cranes at work in the port and ships setting sail.

It also came up during my years in Milan working with Franco
Albini. Albini was a great architect and a man of very few words.
He designed furniture, buildings, "suspended" staircases that
would almost touch the floor, that would brush it ever so lightly

without touching the ground. That was his way of defying gravity, his gamble on lightness.

Lightness has not only a physical dimension but an aesthetic and ethical one. Everyone knows that when it comes to intelligence, there are light touches and heavy hands. A light touch allows you, even at your most determined, to listen to others and seek to understand them. Heavy hands you're better off without.

Lightness is key to understanding places, and, in that sense, an architect must inhabit the places where he works. I have been a Parisian, a Berliner, a New Yorker, a Londoner, and a Kanak. All the while remaining who I am.

I think an architect who does not recognize himself in the place that he is building cannot capture its soul.

Bougna

Kanak culture is ephemeral insofar as it is rooted in performance more than in concrete art and the objects of *coutume*,[6] though the latter exist. Every stone has a name and every tree a story. They are convinced that their ancestors walk alongside them and guide the way, that they are their hidden compass. In a civilization that has never preserved its culture in writing, body language substitutes for books.

Take *pilou*, a traditional dance representing stories of love, cyclones, and battles. All ceremonial functions are accompanied by music played with conch shells and bamboo flutes. When the center opened to the public, the Kanak, so I have been told, put on a memorable show. I wasn't there, but the Explorer attended the ceremony.

---

[6] *Coutume*, or rituals, here refers to the rules governing coexistence, keeping one's word, ancestral customs, ways of living, and the exchange of gifts.

The culture expresses itself through movement. Indeed, at the inauguration they performed a dance I will never forget.

In the outdoor amphitheater overlooking the lagoon, in total silence, they had undertaken the patient task of packing the dirt, to be used as a drum.

The performers danced, stomping the ground with their bare feet, a hundred of them at the same time. It was as if they could transfer the sound that penetrated the earth out to the water and back again. Or else they jumped in unison and suddenly everything trembled. The ground itself is the Kanak drum.

There are many extraordinary facts about the Kanak people, which we do not have the time or competence to enumerate. In the villages, each family has its own home, yet there is no such thing as private property. The huts and land belong to all the members of the tribe. An example of this is *bougna*,[7] which they eat with their hands out of the same pot.

We arrive at the port in the dark of night. The boatswain gives orders to dock. The lines are tossed out to shore where the mooring crew attaches them to the bollards. Electric cables and a water hose are unraveled and connected to water and electricity dispensing columns. The stern and bow of the ship are secured to the quay. The topside of the *Magnaghi* leans into the pier fenders, and the fenders groan. They seem to be complaining about the donkey work that is their lot.

Song of the Huts

But that is not the only noise that can be heard on this warm night. There is another sound, a cross between a whistle and a melody. Even my father hears it, and he's half deaf.

---

[7] A soup made with fish, root vegetables, potatoes, and yams.

It is the huts singing. Every building in the Pacific sings.

In this part of the world the trade winds blow nonstop for five months out of the year, always in the same direction, at twenty knots.

That was what gave us the idea of playing with the wind and its sounds, using wood as our building material. Which is why our cultural center sings when the air passes through it.

It helped us to observe what the Kanak and the Australian Aboriginals and the Maori have always done: they build their music-making houses to emit sounds when the breeze flows through them.

We also worked on the visual vibration of the surface. The façade exposed to the wind was made of strips of wood that spread out as they rise, creating a gradual transition for the air in order to block the wind and avoid turbulence. Standing in the way of the wind creates eddies, as anyone who sails is well aware. You need to let them flow a little. And that is what produces that sound.

All of this intense activity went into designing the shells, a mix of history, science, and this enchanting world.

Waking up on the sheltered bay of Nouméa, no longer surrounded by an endless stretch of water, sets one right with the world. It gratifies the part of us that is earthbound. There is an explosion of colors. Women wear colorful flowers in their black hair. The Kanak flag flapping above the port authority bears the same colors: blue for the Pacific hugging the archipelago, red for the blood spilled in the war of independence, green for the woods that is home to their ancestors. On the left side of the flag is a yellow circle symbolizing the blazing sun and, inside the circle, a strange drawing, a kind of totem depicting the ornate finials that adorn the roofs of huts in New Caledonia, known as *flèches faîtières*. Many of these emblems of clans and clan pride are beautiful. Somewhat like the brass plaques on front doors in Italy. *Flèches faîtières* also keep bad spirits away, like tabernacles with statues of the Madonna.

From the city center, with its colonial-style houses and boulevards lined with palm trees, you can see the Tina Peninsula. Facing us are the ten shell-like huts of the Tjibaou Center, all different sizes. The wood of the curved ribs is gray, like the trunks of Cook pine. The Constructor chose to use Iroko, a moisture-resistant wood from Ghana that, most importantly, cannot be digested by termites.

Arrived in Tina, we are now at a far remove from the city life of Nouméa, catapulted into another realm as we walk the trail that curves around the inlet, bordered by an array of mangroves. There are also large banyan trees, underneath which the dead are buried, and terraces made of taro, and fields of yams and amborella, the oldest flowering plant.

The ten huts, with their tie rods and bolts in plain view, look incomplete. An elderly Kanak who had visited the space when the first shell was finished once said that it reminded him of a hut from his village, only one in the process of being built, one still missing its straw roof. "We're not us anymore," he said, "but we're still us."

Sounds enigmatic, yet his words capture the suspended state of a people torn between tradition and modernity, determined to defend their twenty-nine languages yet forced to speak French to communicate, who fight for their autonomy yet vote to remain an overseas territory, who embrace the future yet cling to their ancestral roots.

My father is lost in thought as he stares at the smooth surface of the Tina lagoon. A worm, or a termite, is gnawing at him. He had chased Atlantis here too. You can't call the huts he built ugly. They quiver and hum in the trade winds, combine stone and wood with modern materials, attract thousands of visitors. They're beautiful.

Beauty is something you look for everywhere, even unconsciously, day and night. You look for it in the light and in the dark, in silence and in words, in music, in film, in art, in natural landscapes. You look for it in the company of others and in the eyes of others. The human species naturally aspires to beauty. It is the tireless engine of our desires.

Nice words, but something is off. What is bothering him? He doesn't answer and continues to stare at the mangroves. I wonder if the huts aren't too much like the huts in the villages, if the allusion lapses into romanticism. They look more like the work of an anthropologist than an architect, as if the real *J* designer had been Bensa. One senses the (slightly superficial) myth of the noble savage. Minutes pass before he makes up his mind. "Hmph," is all he says. Then silence again.

What does that mean? I'm not going to insist he say.

A century and a half ago, the schooner *Academy* was sailing in the same spot we are now navigating on a rainy December afternoon with fair, eleven-knot winds. It was a ship, a natural sciences laboratory, and a floating museum. Docked in San Francisco during the off-season, it would invite the public to marvel at its discoveries.

We're en route to California. We will sail past the shores of Fiji and the Polynesian kingdom of Tonga, stopping in Hawaii before launching straight, in a single crossing, for Frisco Bay.

I have spent the last several days talking at length with *baccan* Pasculli. His favorite subject is, no surprise, the ship. It's practically his sweetheart. He told me about the career of the *Magnaghi*, which first set sail from Riva Trigoso in 1975. But it still has lots of saltwater to cross before it enters dry dock to be dismantled. I hadn't known that steel from retired military ships was sold to razor-blade manufacturers—therefore recycled. One day you might find yourself shaving with the frigate *Maestrale*.

The captain enumerated the latest missions of the A5303 crew. They have been in the Gulf of Pozzuoli to study underwater volcanic eruptions; in Panarea, where gas bubbles were released from the depths; in the Cinque Terre Marine Reserve to hunt for microplastic contaminants. The crew has conducted research campaigns on shipwrecks in the Tyrrhenian and hydrographic surveys in the Strait of Sicily, or, as the French and Tunisians call it, the Canal de Kélibia. For centuries people in the Mediterranean have called places by different names, much to people's confusion.

To reach California, the *Magnaghi* will have to travel over five thousand miles. At a cruising speed of twelve knots, the trip will take us about four hundred hours. Depending on the currents and winds. We expect to reach dry land just before Christmas.

Certainly we will be docking in Honolulu to stock up on supplies and, most importantly, refuel, seeing as the maximum range is four thousand miles. According to navy rules, navy ships have to carry at least half a tank of fuel at all times, in case of emergencies.

Hall of Monsters

In the summer researchers from the California Academy of Sciences used to set sail for the Galapagos, the ecosystem that inspired Darwin, and sometimes they would travel on to Madagascar. In both places, they studied plants and animals. Though the Academy's museum eventually washed up in the heart of Golden Gate Park, they have never stopped exploring.

They continue to organize expeditions and discover hitherto unknown species or species thought to be extinct, like the Fernandina giant tortoise, the pink-headed duck of Myanmar, the Wondiwoi tree kangaroo, the Himalayan quail, and the harlequin frog from the Venezuelan forest.

The Explorer turns up the collar of his peacoat to cover his white beard. A blue beanie covers the rest of his head. He looks like a character out of *Captains Courageous*. The blasts of air from the dock have become unbearable.

The museum was never just some display cabinet. Exploration was always wedded to popularization. The museum

remains invested in research and employs hundreds of full-time scientists.

I remember visiting the vaults before the start of the project. There was a laboratory full of strange instruments and two ethologists who specialized in cobras. They told me they spent three months a year traveling the world, reaching the wildest places by canoe or tramping through the jungle.

A little later on I found out that one of them, Joseph Slowinski, was bitten in Myanmar while studying a type of yellow-and-black-striped krait snake that he had discovered. An antidote for its poison had yet to be invented. Nothing could be done. The rescue helicopter was grounded on account of monsoons, and Joseph died at base camp thirty hours after being bitten.

I immediately took up with these scholars. They were extraordinary people, ready to risk their lives to shed light on the mysteries of nature. To this day the Academy has retained the adventurous character of its heyday.

The Academy didn't make landfall in Golden Gate Park until the turn of the twentieth century. Since then its scientists have collected twenty million species of animals and plants. That may sound like a lot, but it is only five percent of all species in existence.

During that visit, the director, Patrick Kociolek, a scientist who specializes in diatoms, and John McCosker, who studies the evolution of aquatic animals, walked me through the labyrinthine halls of their storage facility, which houses twenty million species.

In a hall over a hundred meters long, thousands of fish were preserved in jars of formaldehyde. Every jar held a different fish. They looked as if they were alive. They seemed to be watching me. The ones from the deep sea were monsters. But I was told not to worry, for there's nothing as dead as a dead fish.

The sight was terrifying, but what they told me was worse.

Identified species make up barely a twentieth of those existing and those lost, about which we still know nothing. Often, these species are invisible to the naked eye or reside in the deep reaches of the sea.

Just in the last year researchers from the Academy have added over a hundred species, including anthropoids, plants, reptiles, and amphibians. They found a lizard with green blood on the islands of São Tomé and Príncipe, and a white-striped frog that has inhabited the Ngozi Crater in Tanzania for a hundred million years. Not that anyone ever noticed.

The Albatross

At some point the museum no longer had a home, or rather it had more than one, but all of the buildings had been damaged by a magnitude 7.1 earthquake. On October 17, 1989, the area around San Francisco was struck by the Loma Prieta earthquake. Once again, the San Andreas Fault had shifted. Several years after the disaster, they contacted my father. Well, his and three other architecture firms.

While we are talking, the rain lets up. The sky, an increasingly lighter shade of gray, fills with flocks of ash-colored birds, some flying so close to the ground they almost skim our radar. They make various shapes in the air, catching the updrafts to rise and plummet. I have never seen these birds before, but our head chef Savasto has. They are terns, birds that navigate by the stars. At this time of year, they migrate to California to nest. A mysterious natural order compels them to cross the ocean.

Like the solitary albatross, which makes a smooth landing on water but struggles to take flight again. From above, the *Magnaghi* must look small, a white spot in the ripples of water.

I'm fascinated by the albatross, by this large bird that manages to go around the world and rarely descends to the water to feed. It has a superficial view, a bird's-eye view, as it were. The albatross scans the sea and plunges when it catches sight of fish. Then it does break the surface, seizing its prey as long as the sea isn't calm, otherwise it could never take off again.

The albatross only hunts when the waves are big enough to act as a trampoline and it can take advantage of the currents that form on the surface. In a poem by Baudelaire, a group of sailors pokes fun of an albatross that has settled on their deck. With his gigantic wings, the "king of the azure" moves awkwardly, almost comically on boat and dry land.

An albatross has a wingspan of over three meters and weighs at least twelve kilos when dry and as much as fifty wet. It could never take flight again without a push from the waves. And when that push comes, the bird launches out, flaps its wings hard and takes off as quickly as possible.

Tell me, Carlo, do you know of a more intelligent animal? One more capable than the albatross of combining superficiality and profundity?

Such is life; in my work I realize how fundamental a bird's-eye view is, how necessary it is to see the big picture in order to understand where I ought to probe further.

But a surface-level view isn't necessarily superficial. We're all a bit condemned to superficiality; we sense we are incapable of understanding the world. So, we run for cover, occasionally diving into the depths like the albatross.

I suppose it is that sense of inadequacy that makes us restless. The imperfection that we are confined to live with compels us to seek Atlantis. And maybe the fact that Atlantis remains shrouded in mystery is a good thing. Maybe it never existed yet exists in every place. It embodies the perfection which we long for and will never realize. What we do is always lacking something, and we are perfectly aware of that fact.

Some Say No

My father knows it. Otherwise he would never have been so stubborn about pursuing this—senile, I presume—mania for Atlantis. This adventure that has us bouncing around the world, chasing chimeras. First in the Southern Hemisphere and now in North America, where he has built a lot. Not just in Frisco but in Boston, Chicago, Dallas, Houston, Los Angeles, and New York.

The offer to participate in the design competition for the Academy came attached with images of the old museum, a group of twelve buildings inside the park. All of them had been built between 1916 and 1991, a row of lots placed in no particular order that had been half-destroyed or at least damaged by the quake. They weren't sure how to fix the problem, but I was working on other projects at the time, and when I'm working on something, I'm like a kid: completely absorbed.

My father always says no at first, whether it concerns a design project or another matter. His refusals must be taken with a grain of salt.

Saying no is part of his playbook. When a new job presents itself, he says he has other things to do. He's not lying, but he often ends up doing the job anyway. To convince him to build the church of Padre Pio in San Giovanni Rotondo, the then treasurer of the Capuchin friars, Father Gerardo, sent him a fax every morning with a personal blessing. After all those prayers, my father converted. He changed his mind about the California Academy too, but had it not been for a solemn commitment to my sister Lia, he may never have accepted the job. He had promised to take her around the world. Though I don't think they ever completed the trip, they did get as far as San Francisco.

One Sunday they took a walk in the green rectangle of Golden Gate Park. The same park where the Summer of Love had launched the countercultural movement, where flower children had blossomed and withered, where the Berkeley student protests against the Vietnam War had broken out. Home of the Beat Generation, the fight for gay rights, Kerouac's *On the Road*, the music of the Grateful Dead. The city was also the birthplace of environmentalism, the Sierra Club having been established there by the revolutionary John Muir. At the end of the nineteenth century Muir was already guarding the Californian mountain ranges against developers and lobbying for nature reserves. My father claims that he would never have constructed that building had it not been in Frisco, which has always been a pioneer in sustainability.

He and Lia spent an afternoon in the botanical gardens and fields of eucalyptus, sequoias, and Monterey pines. They talked about how the weather was mild but the air damp. It is a strange climate; in the summer, mists rise off the ocean, spill down the side of the hills and by morning blanket the city.

They lingered in the middle of the lush green park, which, however, isn't natural. It seems like a contradiction, but it's the truth. This part of California has little surface water and, to irrigate the tall trees, water has to be pumped up from the phreatic zone.

It was totally by chance. I hadn't drawn up a plan to participate in the competition. We simply spent three days in California because it was on the way to Australia, New Caledonia, and Japan, where we were headed.

But, after that stroll in the park, I realized the competition was interesting. The buildings were at the center of Golden Gate

Park. Building and park were born at the same time. I was struck by how deeply rooted in the past they were. You could sense the history in the buildings and stones, and also in the people we encountered outside the Academy.

Grandparents with their grandchildren were making the same visit they had made as fathers and, even earlier, as sons. As a European and Italian, I was familiar with being tugged between preserving the memory of a place and needing to reinvent, with keeping a record of the past and uncovering something new.

To truly create something, an architect must accept the contradictions of his profession: discipline and freedom, nature and technology, memory and invention. He appreciates the past yet also loves to experiment, to explore the future.

Untangling these knots can be complicated, even for me. Because the culture of the past threatens to bury you under an avalanche of memories, especially if you were born in Italy. The grand tradition is a paralyzing force. Borges put it better than I can when he said that creative work is suspended between memory and oblivion. We need to remember many things, not everything. Luckily.

Sometimes even young people are seized by nostalgia for an idealized past. And you know what the danger is? Immobility. There is a small detail that I always try to bear in mind: the past may be a fine refuge, but the one place we can go is toward the future.

Do you remember the words with which F. Scott Fitzgerald concludes *The Great Gatsby*? "So we beat on, boats against the current, borne back ceaselessly into the past."

The waves are rising, the wind brisk. According to Chief Petty Officer Gianfelice Mulas, it was the Brisa blowing, a harsh northeasterly wind that spends all winter whizzing around Makin and Butaritari, in the Gilbert Islands. In the waters of Honolulu they call this threat *pali*, which funnels through the mountains before pouring out to sea. Near the coast of California we will run up against the Coromuel winds, but what worries him is the Cordonazo, which travels up from Mexico and often brings with it hurricanes.

But we can rest easy, because the Cordonazo turns rough a little before or a little after the Feast of Saint Francis, and October 4 had already come and gone. My father, frozen by the winds, picks up the thread of his discussion.

What were we talking about? Ah, yes, my first visit with Lia to the museum in San Francisco.

Through the glass I saw laboratories packed with people engaged in conversation, explaining and listening to one another. I thought the building itself could become an object of study for naturalists, a container that was itself contained, an example of sustainability and respect for nature.

So, the following day, I met with the heads of the Academy. It was worth it.

The Tonga Trench

Giobatta is making his rounds on the deck. He has to check that nothing is out of place, that the *Magnaghi* can travel safely on. Boatswains have a lot of responsibility; should the captain go missing or be otherwise incapacitated, command of the ship falls to the officials, in order of rank, and then to him. Checking to make sure the ties of the lifeboat are nice and tight and the anchor secure in the hawsepipe, he asks, "Do you know how many meters of water we have under the keel?" I have no idea. Luckily, he answers his own question. "10,882. We're over the Tonga Trench, the deepest after the Mariana. That trench is 10,994 meters deep." Our latitude is 22°56'41" South, our longitude 174°43'59" West.

The crew knows all about these deep ocean trenches. It is their job to plumb them. The first descent of the Mariana was achieved by the Swiss-designed, Italian-built bathyscaphe, *Trieste*. It touched down on January 23, 1960, at 1:06 P.M., carrying two men on board, including the oceanographer Jacques Piccard. Down there they saw transparent shrimp and flat fish; the bottom resembled a desert with bright microalgae. Those microalgae were diatoms, the same single-celled organisms studied by Kociolek, who met my father that Monday along with the board of the Academy.

I arrived alone and entered a very large room. The tables were arranged in a circle, as if for an exam, and I was to sit in the middle and display my ideas. The very first thing I did was ask if we could change the seating arrangement and push the tables together so that we could look one another in the eye. During the course of the project, my debut became an anecdote of near mythic proportions.

I admit I was pleasantly surprised by the fact that Kociolek, with whom I would collaborate for five years, was a scientist. I had brought nothing specific with me, no design. I am loath to present a design without first having seen a place with my own eyes. During the meeting we began to talk. All I had with me was a sheet of paper where I was making little sketches. I asked questions, tried to understand.

He appreciated it, since I was adopting his own method, that of an observer. All scientists begin by making observations. He told me that observing is as important as understanding. The idea of working with a man of science appealed to me.

The meeting had been organized to interrogate me, but by the end we were all interrogating the future of the Academy.

I did not start to design the Academy until I had walked around the place once more, listened to its sounds again, taken measurements. One of the first sketches was a kind of diagram of the roof at the same height as the existing edifice.

The Smell of Salt

He and my sister were supposed to hit every continent on their trip. The Surveyor had also promised to take me on a trip around the world, after my graduation. But then I joined the editorial staff of a paper in Milan, first writing articles about local news and then stories of slightly greater importance. There were my colleagues' drafts to edit, titles and taglines to come up with. It was a small paper and it took everything we had to put it out. So because of me we skipped the adventure. But we are making our grand tour now, thirty years later, aboard this ship. Maybe it's better this way; we have more time to talk and reflect and, if anything, bump heads.

Accompanying us are the smells of the sea. In the middle of the Pacific the dominant odor is dried salt. There are also particles of plankton and mollusks, and the smells carried on the wind. A bouquet of deserts, forests, icebergs, and cities. Buenos Aires, Sydney, and Frisco too.

My father made two discoveries on his visit to the old museum. One below ground and one above: on the climb down to the bottom floor, where the fish in formaldehyde eyed him, and on the climb up to the rooftop. Walking on the roof, he expected the building to soar above the park. The trees are very tall, so even on the roof he found himself immersed in nature.

But that vegetation had nothing to do with the original flora. On the day the Academy opened, a Native American, a descendent of the people who owned the land, performed a ritual in which he fanned smoke in the direction of the building using a hawk's wing. He said that the plot of land belonging to his ancestors had been made good use of, that it was the one remaining patch of *native* California, since the bushes we planted on the roof were the same that had grown there two centuries before.

The Ohlone tribe lived there. Literate or not, they were certain that if they respected nature, nature would reward and protect them. The planet, as the Ohlone already knew, is fragile.

Plastic Patch

The earth is fragile, the sea more so. Even in the open sea we come across plastic bags floating on the surface. Every time the boatswain sees one, he curses. He's right. We treat the sea like our dumping ground.

In the middle of the South Pacific is the uninhabited island of Henderson. It belongs to the Pitcairn Islands, famous for having been a refuge for the mutineers of the *Bounty*. Millions of pieces of plastic are deposited on its shores: there's an average of seven hundred scraps per square meter. The cause? The convergence of the currents here and the Great Pacific Garbage Patch, an enormous buildup of floating debris that expands and contracts from 135° to 155° West and 35° to 42° North.

"You've never seen the Patch? I have, and it's really freaky," says Ensign Frascaro. The patch does not appear on the maps, he explains. He had brushed by it once, on board the aircraft carrier *Garibaldi*. They had been sailing between Hawaii and California, traveling in the same direction. It's an immense gyre of bottles, balloons, bags, lighters, syringes, and fishing nets.

The plastic patch can't be picked up by satellite; you need to pass by it to know it exists. The first person to detect it, twenty years ago, was a boat captain named Charles Moore.

Moore was returning to the continent in his catamaran, *Algalita*, after a regatta. He was in no hurry, so he decided to deviate off course. He sailed north into a seldom-traveled area known for calm air and high pressure. In fact, sailboats have long avoided it, and sailors call it the "horse latitudes," since you need a team of them to haul you across the flat sea.

Moore discovered the patch that day. We don't know exactly how vast it is, but it is at least as big as the Iberian Peninsula. We do know that it can grow, even double in size, depending on the play of gyres and sea flows.

Changes

The days on board slip by as we idle, rocking back and forth, changing shifts. They are punctuated by onboard routines and surprise drills ordered by Captain Pasculli. We learn how to treat wounds, put out a fire in the engine room, rescue a drifting shipwreck.

The stories we tell at sea are stories we'd never tell on dry land, as if the boat were a confessional. We confide in one another. Maybe because time goes by so slowly. Rhythms drag. Long, drawn-out silences become more frequent. "We're all in the same boat" is not just a figure of speech.

The Surveyor is neither busy nor irritable, as he can be in the chaos of his studio. He listens and speaks. With a little patience you can even interrogate him.

It struck me as appropriate that the seat of a natural sciences institute should become a symbol of the environmental crisis. In part because a change of mindset was taking place, and the center was in San Francisco, long the cradle of American ecology.

The planet's fragility, the need to establish an intelligent relationship with the environment, was beginning to dawn on us. I was fascinated by the idea of working that way, using nature while surrounded by nature. It meant respecting fauna and flora, correctly arranging the buildings and plants, taking advantage of the light and wind.

The world goes on changing, and those changes are often sudden and unexpected. If an architect does not get lost in the vagaries of style, he senses those changes and translates them into brick and mortar. By a strange twist of fate I found myself not changing the world, obviously, since the world changes on its own, but giving those changes material form. We are living through an age of the most rapid transformations in recorded history: a revolution in geopolitics, customs, habits, scientific discoveries.

Society, history, people, and communities evolve, sometimes by violent ruptures. That was true of Beaubourg, which somehow grew out of the climate in Paris in 1968, but it wasn't the building that changed the culture. Clearly the times demanded a response to the idea that cultural places were the exclusive preserve of the elite; it was time to open them to everyone. Beaubourg picked up on a need that was just. That has been the case for many of my projects.

And that is why, sometimes, buildings aren't grasped at first, because the changes have yet to be grasped. You can't expect widespread acclaim. Being an architect is not an easy profession.

I have had that sensation very often. In 1989 the Berlin Wall fell, and two years later I was called in to work on Potsdamer Platz. You find yourself at a crucial moment in time giving architectural form to an historic turning point. I also constructed the first skyscraper in New York after September 11. That too signaled a change: the choice of transparency as an element of security. It is happening again in Uganda, where I am currently building a pediatric hospital with Gino Strada and EMERGENCY, the humanitarian NGO. People rush to associate Africa with tragedy, poverty, and neglect, but Africa is also a proving ground of opportunity and energy. That is one change underway.

The same was true for the California Academy, which understood and interpreted the vulnerability of our planet. For the culture of construction, it marked the start of a period of radical transformation. The museum in San Francisco had to become the bearer of that message.

We worked with botanists on building the green roof with California plant life that could survive on the moisture of the climate without our having to pump groundwater to irrigate it. The head botanist was Frank Almeda, a biodiversity specialist, since retired.

We wanted a green living roof that created the best climatic conditions inside the building, which is naturally ventilated. Because it is clear that, aside from being beautiful, a green roof that absorbs moisture at night and releases it during the day has major thermal inertia. It was the first time in America that such a large public structure was built without air conditioning.

In Praise of Theft

The green roof, I say, was not his invention. I'd seen plenty in the countryside. They've been around for centuries; farmers have long known that the earth is a good insulator. We didn't have to wait for him to arrive and explain that to us.

Besides, in recent years, these grass roofs had become all the rage: stuck on a museum in Bonn, a school in Singapore, a hotel in Patagonia, and even on the Parliament House in Canberra. I remind him of that fact while the commander gives the order, as he does every evening, to lower the flag.

Don't talk nonsense!
It isn't some superficial homage to an ideology or fashion of

the day. We created a green roof to save energy, respect the environment, and curb pollution as much as possible. I will admit that I didn't invent anything. I took the idea of an animated living roof, which breathes and converses with its surrounding nature, from very old traditions practiced in houses all around the world.

At night the mound of dirt and layer of vegetation on the roof accumulate moisture, and by day they disperse moisture and heat. Sustainable architecture, governed by need, has been around forever.

I'm sure they gave it their all to do a good job. But I am making a different point. He didn't discover the green roof. Were this a trial, I would accuse him of theft, or at least misappropriation. On top of that, he's bragging about it. He wrinkles his brow. I fear the worst, but he remains unruffled.

What's the big deal?
I've spent my life listening to other people's ideas. And stealing them. Shamelessly, but always out in the open. I've taken from writers, scientists, musicians, filmmakers, artists, educators—everybody. And that's not all. I've pillaged from anyone—mentors, friends, acquaintances—that had an interesting idea. And I have never regretted it, because in the end I pay it all back; if I can, with a little something extra. By building public spaces for people. The important thing is paying it back.

I have always told young architects that come to the studio: Take what you find here and bring it with you, with the understanding that you pay it back with interest. What matters is that you do not shut yourself off in your own world. Don't be a prisoner to yourself. Being an architect is a bit like being a pirate.

Stolen or not, making a green roof was a feat of scientific research. The botanists had to select the plant species that would take root without needing to be watered. An area with the same microclimate was identified thirty kilometers from Golden Gate Park, a sandy windswept hill where they could test which species would ultimately be planted on top of the building. They began with twenty types and whittled it down to nine.

On the roof of the museum, 1,700,000 specimens were planted, all in coconut coir trays that, after rooting, would break down. The forty-five square centimeter trays were made by the botanist Paul Kephart. Plants were chosen for reasons beside their origin: *Prunella vulgaris* because it attracts hummingbirds and hornets. The *Fragaria chiloensis* because it lures wild birds. Moths hover around the pink flowers of *Armeria*, and *Sedum spathulifolium* draws butterflies. Bees love the white, yellow, and orange *Eschscholzia californica*. And *Plantago erecta*, *Lasthenia californica,* and *Layia platyglossa* create a welcome habitat for beneficial insects.

The botanists were not the only ones to collaborate on the design of the Academy; energy scientists were also brought on. Seventy thousand polycrystalline photovoltaic cells produce more than ten percent of the building's electricity, and the walls facing outward provide ninety percent of its light. Radiant heating reduces the building's energy needs by ten percent. In addition, 120 tons of previously demolished building materials were ground down and reused to make concrete. The water in the Aquarium is collected from the Pacific. Ninety-five percent of the steel used is recycled, and eighty-five percent of the insulation is made from recycled blue jeans. The same Levi's that left their mark on the history of San Francisco.

Gold Fever

Our latitude is 37°46'29" North, our longitude 122°25'09" West. We have been sailing for almost a month, stopping for just a couple of days in Honolulu to restock the pantry and refuel.

Savasto, who doesn't lack for imagination in the kitchen, has run out of ideas for new dishes to feed the crew. The result is general disgruntlement. You can't sail well, or think well for that matter, when you don't eat well. The engineers are crabby, the helmsmen testy, the officers addled. As a rule, sailors do not vary their diet. Once upon a time they chugged along on salted beef, hardtack, and potatoes.

We had loaded the ship with what little the general store on the island had to offer: macadamia nuts, pineapples, avocados, and bananas. Luckily we're drawing near the Bay of San Francisco, with its restaurants and supermarkets.

The Sacramento and San Joaquin Rivers drain into the Bay, which, during the Gold Rush, was the most heavily trafficked port in the world. In just one year over seven thousand ships rounded Cape Horn to dock here. Everybody had gone insane. In a few months the population swelled from eight hundred to twenty-five thousand, and saloons, casinos, and brothels followed. The Chinese called this land Jin Shan, or Gold Mountain; the Spanish dubbed it Eldorado; and Italians, ever the good Catholics, named it Paradiso. As one gazette put it, "The whole country . . . from the shore to the base of the Sierra Nevada, resounds to the sordid cry to gold, GOLD, GOLD!" The next day the newspaper shuttered, and its journalists, armed with pickaxes and buckets, flocked to the hills to find nuggets.

Maybe the race for gold to the tune of "Oh! Susanna" was, in its way, a search for Atlantis. But it isn't our search, not as my father intends it. Nor did he ever find Atlantis here, of that I'm certain. Otherwise he would not be talking about setting sail for New York before we've even landed. His Atlantis is not concealed in the clouds now gathering in the bay, to the consternation of *baccan* Pasculli. Many eyes are needed to spot the obstacles that emerge from the haze.

Good ears are needed too. We can hear the sirens wailing at regular intervals from the towers of the Golden Gate Bridge. Maybe the bridge was painted orange to ensure it could be seen in the fog. There are twenty other sirens scattered around the islands and along the coast, each emitting a unique whistle, the one on Alcatraz different from that on Angel Island or Yerba Buena. Like a concert of hisses, emanating from the pipes of an immense organ shrouded in mist.

7.
The Petrified Forest

With the winds of San Francisco at our backs we sail south toward the humid, stifling blanket of Panama. In the Gulf of Parita the sea is flat, or as the boatswain says, a "*mâ*" of turtles and moonfish that only swim to the surface when there is dead calm. We enter the Panama Canal and from here will turn north again, to New York.

I am still thinking of the science academy, crowded with curious kids, kids enchanted by the planetarium and the rainforest biosphere, enthralled by the aquarium and the earthquake simulator. As I expected, no Atlantis. But in the laboratories I saw biologists working with chemists, fossil experts with geologists, physicists, and astronomers explaining the origins of Earth to students.

Botanists and ornithologists recounted the ecosystem of Genovesa, an island inhabited exclusively by birds: frigate birds, lava and swallow-tailed gulls, gannets, common terns, petrels, and Darwin's chaffinches. Working with a team is another of my father's fixations. Second only to taking measurements, perhaps.

Everyone pays lip service to teamwork. But I put teamwork into practice, and always have. I did it with Peter Rice, rapidly ping-ponging between construction, society, and culture. I also worked with Richard Rogers, who taught me many things.

And I continue to practice it at the office, where we volley ideas back and forth in groups of four, six, eight people. The best idea wins, no matter who it comes from, so that, when we have finished, you no longer know who did what. You have to trust those you work with, show them respect, and listen. You argue, sometimes you fight. The most irritating moments are often the most illuminating.

The reason I grew up believing that there is always something to learn from others is quite simple: at school I was a dunce. I couldn't tell you what it's like to grow up at the top of your class, because that was never my experience. But it could not have been all that bad, for other reasons.

Atlantises

To cross the isthmus we had to wait ten hours in the sluices of Gatun Lake and the dam of Miraflores.

In the middle of this stretch of jungle, ships advance slowly, single file, one after the other. There is also a museum that tells the story of the Canal. Panama's motto, *Pro mundi beneficio* (For the Benefit of the World), is fixed above the entrance. This shortcut between the two oceans was coveted back in the days of the *conquistadores*, who were looking for a way to avoid the violent gusts of Cape Horn's williwaw. But they gave up on the idea. It was too ambitious for engineering of the time.

In the days that followed, due to a problem with the bilge pump, we had to dock in San Juan, Puerto Rico. The sailors knew the place, mostly on account of Bacardi, the rum distillery that fled Cuba after Castro's revolution. We tasted various rums with Giobatta: añejo, dorado, overproof, rhum agricole made from pure cane sugar. Each glass was meant to be the last. My head throbbed for the entire journey across the algae of the Sargasso Sea. It wasn't until we had almost reached our destination that my hangover abated. Now we are at latitude 40°42'51" North, longitude 73°56'19" West.

In the distance stands a petrified forest, with skyscrapers for trees. The skyscrapers mirror the countless lives lived there. Stories lurking in the streets and buildings, eyes observing us from millions of windows. This is Manhattan as seen from the bridge of the *Admiral Magnaghi*: a reinforced concrete wood, surrounded by the East River on one side and the Hudson on the other, with sharp peaks and sudden dips.

The Explorer removes a piece of paper from his pocket. Plato again. *Critias*, this time, in which Plato describes the citizens of Atlantis: "As sober men do, they saw clearly that even prosperity is enhanced by the combination of mutual friendship and virtue."[8] I don't know why he's reading it. Sometimes he's strange. But I think it best to talk about Atlantises, plural. Many utopias have sunk into the sea or been erased from the map: the kingdom of Prester John, whom Marco Polo describes in his *Travels*; Thule, the legendary island inhabited by the Hyperboreans; Shangri-La, the lost paradise in the mountains of Tibet; and Antillia, where supposedly a group of Spanish bishops took shelter as they fled from the Moors. Explorers also searched in vain for Satanazes, which the cartographer Grazioso Benincasa placed north of Antillia.

Other undiscovered islands include Drogeo, Bermeja, Agartha, Ogygia, Panchaia, Saint Brendan's Island, Meropis, Mayda, Dulichium, and the Cassiterides, reputed to have sunk into the sea off Cornwall. The list of lands that have been dreamed about, and may actually have once existed, is long. Pierre Benoît, author of the bestseller *Atlantis*, may have been

[8] Plato, *Timaeus and Critias*, translated by Robert Waterfield (Oxford World's Classics, 2008)

on to something: a sunken city should remain shrouded by mystery—that way Atlantis can hide everywhere. Including the Big Apple.

Behold the Statue of Liberty, the first sight to greet the hopeful eyes of immigrants. After completing their transatlantic journey, they were lined up at the immigration station on Ellis Island and (for the purpose of thinning the crowds) screened by doctors before they had even set foot in the building. Millions turned up at the entry port to America. First the Irish, fleeing famine, followed by German dissidents and the Chinese, who carved out a world apart in the form of Chinatown. Then came the Jews from Eastern Europe, driven abroad by Czarist oppression, and Italians, largely composed of starving people in search of a better future. Their backs were marked with chalk indicating who could enter, who had to sit in quarantine, and who would be sent back on the first ship out.

Schist

The Explorer watches the forest of towers on our approach. Soon we'll dock. On board there is the usual frenzy that precedes big events. Astern, ropes are unraveled and readied to be fastened to the bitts, and we are escorted by a tugboat that wheezes its way to the wharf. Flags whip about, and pilots and captains communicate using mysterious signs.

Giobatta never takes his lips off his whistle, while a helmsman from Marghera, Sandro Gavagnin, attaches a line to the ring of a red mooring buoy with a boathook. Battered by waves and lashed by hawsers, the ship booms like a drum. The excitement doesn't affect my father: the freezing cold must have anesthetized him. We'd forgotten about the cold down in the southern seas.

The first time I came here as a young man, I was disoriented and awestruck. I had only seen New York on the big screen, at movie theaters on the outskirts of town.

It is a city born of defiance, including the defiance to build upward, out of necessity. Though building upward was made possible because of the highly durable rock called schist that New York rests on. Cut the stone and you have your foundation.

Men have nature to thank for so many skyscrapers. It provided them with solid ground.

I see long, narrow masses of schist in Morningside Park. The rock emerges out of the deep heart of the land, amid clusters of white locusts. Each mass is like the dark tip of an iceberg, veined with fissures. Great blocks of schist turn up here and there in the meadows of Central Park, too. Schist is part of the metropolis' interior, along with the sewers, the aqueducts, the subway tunnels, the homeless shelters, and the steam drifting up from manholes. The latter call to mind a fire-breathing monster trapped in the belly of the city, or an underground tribe sending smoke signals to the outside world. The Surveyor once excavated the stone of Manhattan to make a vault for a trove of books at the Morgan Library. Was he chasing another Atlantis? One of these days, I'll ask him.

As Captain Pasculli lowers the boarding ramp, the last rays of the sun catch the glass of the skyscrapers and blind us.

New York is a Nordic city enclosed by water. Hence it is a metropolis with a variable, almost atmospheric sky. The light and reflections are never the same. The jagged, vertical skyline captures and reflects light.

It changes rapidly and is metamorphic. After a storm, everything turns blue, and at dusk and on sunny days like today it blazes up into an intense red.

The city is in perpetual transformation, as if time sped by more relentlessly here than elsewhere. On every corner there is a worksite with a construction worker jiggling to a jackhammer. The noise is part of the city's soundtrack, along with car horns and the peals of sirens.

Romantic and, at the same time, buried in flakes of plaster. Someone once said that the drum of the jackhammer is to New York what the chime of Big Ben is to London. The city is a human kaleidoscope, a melting pot of ethnicities where merely crossing the street means crossing over into another language, from Yiddish to Cantonese. Looking out at Manhattan from the port is a game of I spy that never ceases to surprise.

Ellis Island

The immigration officers are meticulous. They take our fingerprints with a scanner, photograph us with a webcam, ask myriad questions. Where are you coming from? What is the reason for your stay? Have you had your measles shot? You almost want to answer, "How about you?" But we get it: it's not every day someone steps off an oceanographic vessel.

Besides, back in the time of Ellis Island, you had to wait forever in a gigantic registry room. As many as 8,000 people were crammed into the room; getting through all the paperwork took at least eight hours. The questionnaire was endless. Women, who were forbidden from traveling alone, were most at risk of being turned down. They had to be accompanied by a man, and those who came to meet their fiancées were obligated to marry the moment they set foot on American soil. Otherwise they were held on Ellis Island, where 350 babies were born, since not all husbands-to-be were in a hurry to claim them.

We raced up to the zoo that is Times Square in a rickety taxi, all potholes and sharp brakes. Times Square is named after the *New York Times*; the gray lady was headquartered here until the tower designed by my father was built, just off Broadway, on 8th Avenue, between West 40th and West 41st.

Generally speaking, around 2000, the whole publishing world was transforming, including the *New York Times*. The digital revolution, which isn't over yet, was in full swing. Papers were no longer printed in basements, the rotary presses had all been relocated outside the city, gone were the days of trucks loaded with freshly inked copies, which left the editors' room at dawn to reach newsstands, airports, and train stations. Arthur Sulzberger Jr. had just taken the helm. New and different spaces were called for to find another way to run a newspaper.

The newspaper was turning into an information hub for all kinds of media, not just print. The first three floors of the tower, which opened onto a central patio, were reserved for the bustling newsroom.

Joe Lelyveld[9] and I used to call it the Bakery. It is here that the paper is conceived, written, and put together, sometimes at night; here that the news comes hot out of the oven; here that the news is broadcast to the world.

We are inside the skyscraper.

We stroll through the tiny forest of New Jersey birches in the atrium, a quiet oasis in the deafening city, though even silent places talk.

We only have a few hours of shore leave. We must be back

[9] Joseph Lelyveld was the executive director of the *New York Times* from 1994 to 2001.

on board by seven P.M., as per the captain's orders. But inside the tower, 319 meters to tip and vanishing in the clouds, we have other things on our minds.

Sometimes, in the winter, it will be raining on the lobby level and snowing on the top floor. It is a question of altitude and fluctuations in the temperature. Hop on the elevator and you could find yourself surrounded by snowflakes, yet to melt. But that isn't going to happen today. It's over forty degrees centigrade outside and the twilit sky is bloodshot.

With its geometric façade, the skyscraper seems to mirror the orderly grid of Manhattan. The latticework pattern is almost boring; it's impossible to get lost on the island. The intersecting streets run north–south and east–west. Only Broadway deviates from the grid, cutting across it diagonally, but Broadway retraces the route of an old Native American path.

Are you asking me where the idea for this tower came from?

Accepting the rules of the game, I think. Immediately and without much hesitation we focused on the urban fabric. Another element is the light: I had always seen New York as a kind of litmus paper: its verticality makes it photosensitive.

But there were two other considerations. First, that the headquarters of a newspaper must be in dialogue with the city that feeds it. Second, the idea of the bakery, open day and night, where journalists come together and embolden one another.

9/11/2001

Something else happened while construction was underway, something that went beyond the world of media: September 11, 2001. I still have a copy of the *New York Times* with its headline "U.S. ATTACKED" in all caps on the front page.

I was in Manhattan that day, along with my father, Milly, Giorgio, Flora, and Lia. Crowds spilled out into the streets, everyone repeating the same words: "My God!" Everyone gaping at the apocalypse devastating downtown. "My God!" said the Indian taxi driver clasping his turban. "My God!" said the broker on Wall Street clutching his briefcase to his chest, like a child clutching a stuffed animal.

Both were at a loss. Both were staring in shock at the cloud of cement obscuring the sun. Any differences between them vanished. They even looked like one another. Language, profession, clothing, income, religion—none of it meant anything that day in Manhattan.

I remember Mayor Giuliani on TV trying, as best he could, to ease the despair of his fellow citizens, his face wan and streaked with tears. He did his best to say something, but what consolation could he offer? I was petrified, too. Grief shrouded the city. That morning in New York, everyone embraced one another, even strangers, who had suddenly become kin.

People emerged from the pall of plaster, caked in dust, looking like ghosts. Those two vertiginous skyscrapers that had once appeared invincible had collapsed like sandcastles. An acrid smell in the air stung your nostrils and burned your lungs.

People no longer rushed along in the morning as they used to. They didn't even walk, New Yorkers. They were paralyzed: some sat on the curb, some on the hoods of cars stuck in traffic, and others leaned on lampposts.

It felt like the end of the world, like being in a war zone, which I had only heard about from my grandparents. In the days that followed, photographs of the missing covered the walls, illumined by candles that cast a funereal glow over the scene. Yet people didn't give up. They searched for news of their husbands, daughters, or friends who had been passing by the towers at that moment. As time passed, hope gave way to heartbreak, and, underneath those photographs, a carpet of flowers and new candles was lain. Public squares became memorials. Every image told the story of a life cut short. In Union Square someone hung a pair of portraits of two Italians, Elvira Granito and Luigi Arena. A cold blade stabbed the pit of your stomach.

Groups of marines guarded the intersections and stations. They wore helmets, scanned the scene nervously, kept their fingers on the trigger of their assault rifles, as if at any minute the enemy might spring. In front of the mansions on 5th Avenue, armored vehicles replaced limousines. Fear was in the air, it was palpable, you almost suspected it had taken possession of people's minds.

I was interning at the *New York Times* then. They had assigned me to the metro section, local news. Every journalist in the newsroom was a wreck. Everyone knew someone who worked in the Twin Towers, and none knew what had happened to them. Or knew all too well. You just needed to dig beneath the rubble. Obituaries were published for months. The grief was collective.

I am still haunted by the memory of September 11. Even my father, I noticed, was rattled that day.

You were there, your sister Lia was there, and your brother Giorgio was there. The first thing I saw were the images on TV, and, like everyone else, I had the impression I was watching a film. Then I went out into the street.

My office was fifteen blocks from the Twin Towers. I witnessed the collapse, the terror, the people fleeing and huddling together in tears. My memory has congealed around that feeling of bewilderment, my own and others. It awakened in me fears that I had buried and repressed.

Having been born in 1937, on the eve of a major war, I am the child of that kind of disaster. Times were hard then. I was too young to remember anything about the war beside the flash of bombs over the Port of Genoa, on the other side of the hills.

And the muffled sound of airplanes that accompanied them. The roar of the engines and the flash of explosions are the score and backdrop of my memories of the war. To this day, if there are more than two or three planes in the sky, the noise in the background makes me shudder. It all came back to me on September 11, with the jets over my head.

My recollection of the war may be hazy, but I have a very clear memory of what happened after.

With every passing day, week, month, the horror receded and my mother seemed more at ease, my father less taciturn, my sister more beautiful, the streets cleaner, the food better. One day my mother arrived home with a banana. I'd never seen one before. It was utterly fantastic.

During the Christmas of, I believe, 1946, my father took me downtown and bought me a Meccano building set, the kind that came with nuts, bolts, screws, and perforated metal pins. On our return to Pegli by tram, I stood with the box tucked between my knees, afraid someone might steal it.

Every day was a little better than the last, all a little better. And so on for every year after 1945. Then a miracle happens: You grow up with the absurd idea that time will set things right; that as it passes, the world around you will improve. Before you know it, you've grown into an optimist.

You also cultivate a profound sense of pacificism and the firm conviction that building is a gesture toward peace, especially when you build hospitals, courts, schools, museums, libraries— places where people who share the same values congregate. To build is to place faith in the future. It is the opposite of destruction.

To build is to edify, to build up morally.

But let's get back to the tragedy of the Twin Towers. The drama of those days intersected with my work. In fact, I had to meet my client to discuss the fate of the skyscraper.

*

He phoned me just before the network went down, after the Boeing flight crashed into the North Tower. He was in shock. He was sure it would fall, he said. Steel melts at a little over 1,300 degrees centigrade, and an impact of that kind, with a plane full of kerosene flying four hundred kilometers an hour, produces twice that heat. He hoped the people inside realized that. They had to get out right away. But that isn't what happened.

The security systems were only equipped for routine fires, so when they went off, the activated voice told people not to panic, to stay where they were. Only those who disobeyed the order and breathlessly ran down the stairs survived.

Three days later, on September 14, my birthday, I went to dinner with Arthur Sulzberger and Michael Golden, the chairmen of the *New York Times*. There was no guarantee that work on the building would continue.

Some believed you simply could not build a skyscraper again. We talked about what had happened and how it would affect the project. We went back and forth for a long time, and slowly, over the course of our conversation, optimism prevailed.

We agreed that we could not quit the project. And so we spoke a lot about transparency and openness, which would become key qualities of the building.

It is transparency that ensures greater security. Putting up walls and hiding in bunkers is absolutely pointless. It is better to be able to observe and take in what is happening, for prevention's sake too. We all agreed that transparency is not exclusively spiritual or aesthetic; it also serves a practical function.

We believed that the proper response was to do the opposite of what the terrorists wanted us to do: to not hide, to not retreat underground.

The Transparent Bunker

The tower was born at a crucial time, when panic reigned and people expected a fort. But here we are in the airy lobby that, rather than being sealed off, opens out onto the city.

There are no barriers. You can hop from one street to the next by taking a shortcut through the atrium. People are also free to stroll in the garden, as if a piece of New York had slipped inside the building. No one asks to see our ID, even though, after having been so long at sea, we must have looked a fright. With his disheveled, salt-caked hair and his scruffy beard, my father looks like Robinson Crusoe. Nobody recognizes him, and that is for the better.

During that famous dinner the question was: Do we give up on our ideal city? Do we go on lockdown and arm ourselves in the dark? Return to the caves? Adopt the lifestyle of al-Qaeda? Or do we defend our civilization and the city that embodies it?

The barbarity of terrorism attacks a city because, whatever its flaws, a city represents the values of civilization.

The idea of cities does not exist in nature. Cities are an invention, an ancient and splendid one, born of people's need to form community. The Italian words *città* (city) and *civiltà* (civilization) sound alike and have the same root.

That pledge was explicit in Greek *poleis*. Recently elected Athenian politicians took an oath: "I promise, O Athenians, to transmit Athens not only, not less, but more beautiful than it was transmitted to me." More beautiful. Meaning greater.

A city has always been conceived of as a place of contrasts, where experiences merge and fears vanish. As Calvino wrote, there are fragments of happy cities, which even develop within unhappy cities.

We must acknowledge them and make room for them. The city is a site of exchange for goods, dreams, words, cultures, emotions, and memories. Such exchange is facilitated by its density and intensity. The opposite of a city is not the country, which is fertile, but the desert, which produces monsters.

In the Bible, it is the city—luminous, open, shining, hospitable—that embodies humanity's age-old dream: the dream of shalom, or peace. That is the last stop on humanity's journey, about which Cardinal Carlo Maria Martini wrote. As described in the Book of Revelations, the perfect city of the faithful has twelve doors and is 12,000 stadia, or over 2,000 kilometers, in length and width. A metropolis as big as Europe, where all the peoples of Earth are gathered. A territory tamed by mankind—Europe again, which is already one large city. Seen from an airplane, it is a succession of inhabited centers, fertile countryside, woods, rivers, ports, and cities.

Shades of Gray

The clouds paint the news organization a bluish shade of gray. The façade is no longer the same as it was an hour ago; before it was orange. The ceramic pipes take on the color of the light and reflect the qualities of the sky. Not all skyscrapers do. Many are dim and impenetrable. That is not merely a question of style, according to the Constructor.

Do you know why they all have such dark or reflective surfaces?

Because the problem with towers has less to do with heating them up than with cooling them down and shielding them from the sun, so they wind up becoming airtight, mysterious buildings.

That is why we covered the *New York Times* with a lacework of thin ceramic rods which form the vibrant exterior of the building. That idea was nothing new either: keeping out the sun with horizontal slats is a system that our ancestors implemented.

Just think of how shutters are designed. The idea goes way back.

This building is, like the city, photosensitive. We wrapped it in a lacework that is as shimmering and ephemeral as the light.

The natural ceramic exterior takes on different shades of color and is subject to the whims of the weather. It creates emotions with its colors.

We wanted a lively, airy presence that breathed with the wind and changed with the weather. Something firmly grounded and at the same time part of the humus of New York.

What he says is true: it is metamorphic. But the building is more beautiful and less opaque when seen from afar or soaring above the island in a plane. Then, it seems to capture best the moods of the weather. From the street the screen of ceramic rods appears faded, too gray. Some people have joked that the gray is a chromatic allusion to the name the Gray Lady. I know that is not what the Explorer wanted. During the design phase they made dozens of models to choose the right color. It had to be light-colored, not exactly white, but light-colored. Was a mistake made? They were either holding the samples in their hands or had set them on the desk to examine them, so that they were always looking at them from above, at an angle where the light fell. Therefore, the samples appeared bright. Did they overlook the fact that, seen from below, the color would be different? That the lacework would be too dark to reflect the scant light in the shade?

Yes, we got the color wrong, the ceramic should have been lighter. You know perfectly well that no matter what you do there is always something off. There were complaints, even a few hostile reviews. But when a criticism is justified you have to listen and make good use of it.

Very often there is something to be learned, even from the

harshest criticisms. For architects, making a mistake is dangerous, because architecture is a public art and its errors last forever.

There is something else he regrets that he won't admit, something that nags at him. And I know what it is. At the top of the tower, up in the clouds, there was supposed to have been a maple grove from which you could take in the view. Over time the idea was dropped. So, the garden went back in the drawer, and this skyscraper is still waiting for a forest to appear.

8.
THE LIBRARY IN THE STONE

Every once and a while my father is stricken with what physicians call lumbago and what in Italian is commonly known as *colpo della strega*, or witch's stroke. So now the two of us and his back are stuck on board the *Magnaghi*, our flâneuring through the streets of New York on temporary hold, and with it our search for Atlantis. The rain falling in drips from the runners and upper canopy doesn't help. It spatters on the deck and pours into the sea, making concentric circles. And in the meantime it replenishes the Atlantic with fresh water.

Today is a good day to talk. We have taken shelter in the stern cockpit. He is sitting on a kind of director's chair that he brings on sailboats, too, usually placing it on deck, under the boom.

The forest of towers is reflected in the water of the port, reminding us that we are on an island. Underneath, the giant plate of schist props up the skyscrapers.

Yes, New York rests on extremely durable rock, and I think that durability has affected every moment of the city's life and history.

Where you see dense clusters of skyscrapers, the stone is closer to the surface. You go from five meters below the surface at Times Square to eighty below in Greenwich Village. That explains why there are no towers in the Village, only the kind of lowrises you expect to find in a small town.

One thing that has rarely been done is to build by drilling down. But with the Morgan Library—a library interred in rock, an upside-down skyscraper—the Explorer embarked on a voyage to the center of the earth. They excavated stone for nine months.

An architect has two ways of defying nature: either ascend and clash with the force of gravity or descend and collide with the grit of the earth, which here is very compact volcanic rock.

We dug a hole twenty meters deep, cutting into stone just thirty centimeters away from the adjacent buildings, for space is a rare and precious commodity in New York.

From the port you cannot make out the Morgan Library, which faces Madison Avenue between 36th and 37th Street, because it is practically a mine. The part that protrudes is small, nearly insignificant in this city of giants, and our view is obscured by the curtain of rain pouring from the sky.

This is another absolutely ancient idea, like burying treasure. The point was to preserve and protect manuscripts in an underground vault.

The foundations of the Morgan are the soul of the building; they are not merely there to hold it up. They represent its essence.

The Robber Baron's Treasure

Once the Explorer gets going, it is hard to hold him back. The Morgan is the third major depository of books in the world, after the Vatican Museums and the British Library. It has everything from the Gutenberg Bible to a thirteen-year-old Mozart's sheet music. It contains the manuscript of Mark Twain's *Pudd'nhead Wilson*, the pages on which Dickens wrote

✓

A Christmas Carol, an autographed manuscript of Bob Dylan's "Blowin' in the Wind," letters of George Washington, drawings by Michelangelo, and original texts by Galileo and Edgar Allan Poe.

Let's begin at the beginning. When they offered me the job of expanding the Morgan Library, the first thing I did was call Umberto Eco.

He had told me about this library in the heart of Manhattan, and, being a scholar, was enthralled by it. He told me I had to accept. It was an opportunity I could not pass up. He practically ordered me to do it. But if you do, he said, you must not ruin the existing buildings around it.

The three buildings to be preserved were the original 1906 library designed by Charles McKim; the Annex built in 1928, when the collection was opened to the public; and the Morgan family house, an 1852 brownstone. It was the first house in the city to have electricity. John Pierpont Morgan engaged Thomas Edison himself to install it.

The rain, drawn and slant, slips down the collar of his peacoat, but the Old Man pays no attention. He continues to talk about the thousands of tons of schist extracted from the crater and the hundreds of trips needed to truck it away. The Morgan, he explains, was closed to the public until 1928. What was the point of a library, I wonder, if no one could consult it?

Jack Morgan waited several years after the death of his father to open the library to researchers and New Yorkers.

Pierpont was a learned man, yes, but along with the Rockefellers and Vanderbilts, he remained a robber baron. Inside his house, which was also the office where he conducted business, he amassed a fortune of hundreds of thousands of prints, rare books, artworks, drawings, and ancient seals.

They served to show off his power and wealth and overawe his interlocutors. To gain psychological advantage, intimidate visitors. His empire was founded on the rock-hard idea of private property; clearly, he hadn't bought those masterpieces to share them with others. One of his most famous sayings was "If you have to ask, you can never afford it."

Maybe I'm wrong, maybe there was more to him. Maybe, despite being a ruthless businessman, J.P. Morgan really did love art. Still, no one had access to his collection. The human mind is complicated.

Memory and Oblivion

He rises to stretch his legs and inches across the thin strip of deck spared from the downpour.

I had known Umberto Eco. As soon as he saw an opening, he would talk about books, writers, libraries. At his house in Milan's Piazza Castello, he had assembled his own collection of fifty thousand titles. On second thought, it was not so much a house as it was a library where he had carved out a space to live. Everyone who paid him a visit, upon seeing those endless bookshelves, which even invaded the bathroom, would ask if he had read them all.

Eco had a ready answer. "No," he would say, "I keep the ones I've already read at the university. These are the ones I have to read by next week." He had even calculated how much time it would take to read all the books of some importance, allowing four days per volume. Four days for every text worthy of interest would amount to 65,400 days. Divided by 365, that comes out to 180 years.

Therefore, he concluded, no one had ever read, nor could ever read, all the works that matter.

Eco and I discussed the idea of exploration, of descending underground to search for books. At that moment the vision of a vault, of buried treasure, began to take shape. Because that was what we were dealing with: protecting the patrimony that the banker had amassed for himself and making it available to everyone in a civic space.

Eco reminded me about Borges' story, "The Library of Babel," which I read and reread on the plane to New York, where I had an appointment to meet Charlie Pierce, the president of the Morgan. Borges' infinite library is a beautiful idea. Each room is a hexagon and from any point you can see the floors above and below. All books are housed there, those already written and those yet to be written.

Borges, the man of memory and oblivion . . .

Him exactly. It was Borges who said creative work hovers between memory and oblivion. We remember many things, but thankfully not everything. If we did, we'd end up as alienated as Funes, the Memorious. It is profoundly true that creation is a bit of a balance between the many things you recall, the many you have forgotten, and the many you never knew.

So it falls to you to make do, fumble around in the dark, invent from scratch. Memory provides the rules and structure, yet within memory lie the gaps in which you work. But memory must not be overdetermining, otherwise it becomes a prison.

I think it was the saxophonist Charlie Parker who said, "Master the music, master your instrument, and then forget all that and just play."

There was a riddle to solve with the Morgan. They wanted to enlarge the library, but you couldn't without encroaching upon the surrounding space already occupied by streets and other buildings. You had to stay within the perimeter of the building.

In fact, the one solution was to dig and search for space underground. The rock can be cut vertically with scalpel precision. Down below you can carve out an ideal place to preserve cultural patrimony, shielding it from the passage of time, weather events, vandalism.

So, after having determined that there were no aquifers or fractures in the rock, we dug a large pit where we could install this vault of precious books, as well as the facilities and performance hall. I like to compare the building to an iceberg.

Icebergs again! I said it before: he's obsessed with icebergs. But he isn't listening to me. He's following his own train of thought.

There is the part of the iceberg above the surface and the other, no less important, part that remains hidden. I like the idea that one of the most prestigious libraries in the world guards its codices in a cube set in stone.

Libraries, like museums, are preservation factories: they preserve works for eternity. They rescue them from the ravages of time. What I mean to say is that the choice to dig a hole in the earth to preserve books is not only rational but profoundly meaningful. There are things you don't see but know are there. Walking on top of a treasure chest is a wonderful feeling.

Museums like preservation factories? His back permitting, tomorrow we plan to visit the Whitney, just a step away from where the *Magnaghi* is moored.

Of course. A museum rescues works from the wear of time. It is also a factory that generates curiosity and critical awareness. And it is a fortress, too, defending the physical integrity of art in order to pass it down to the future.

Same as the art collections in stately mansions, which once

served to protect paintings from barbarian invasions, whether from near or far. In short, a museum creates durability, cultural durability, physical durability.

Elevator of Regrets

They needed to be careful, as Eco had urged, not to ruin the historic buildings. They were not to be demolished or altered. Unlike the buildings in San Francisco, they had not been damaged by an earthquake. Just as we cannot reset the clock by destroying the past, we cannot rip the pages from a history book only because we wish it were different.

Demolition is a cry of powerlessness. The gesture seems spectacular but is actually rhetorical. Nothing is beyond hope. Starting over from scratch is almost always a big mistake. Cities transform, grow, and live in flux.

The New York rain isn't letting up. Umbrella sellers have materialized on every street corner. Who knows where they keep them when the sun is shining. Where do they fetch them up so quickly, at the first drop of rain? All I know is that after a storm the trashcans are filled with umbrellas. They are short-lived, defeated by the wind. My father resumes talking.

I was saying that the choice to move underground was also dictated by our desire not to overshadow the existing edifices, which are small historic buildings. We had to construct six thousand square meters, and building a high-rise would have disrupted the original nucleus of the library.

So three new units were carefully inserted amid the old, without so much as brushing them, because we left a gap between one building and another: alley-size interstices, a little more than two meters wide.

They might put you in mind of a Genoese *caruggio* or Venetian *calle*. That is how the Morgan was completed without damaging what was there already, letting some air in, making it visible and transparent from Madison Avenue. Visitors must not forget that they are in the middle of a living, breathing city—you cannot leave that energy at the door.

What was originally a place for a select few became open and accessible to all.

And then there is the plaza in the center, the piazza. In Italy, even the tiniest village has a piazza with a town hall and church. Piazzas go by various names: *largo, campo, piazzetta, piazzale, spianata, spiazzo*. A piazza also stands for people, for a place to come together. A piazza is a place to protest, sell goods, and gather to celebrate. A piazza is a place for rallies, races, and markets. Once upon a time duels were held in them, at dawn. A piazza is a fulcrum of dialogue, and life revolves around it. People are obliged to cross it, and there they slow down and stop, linger and encounter others.

With the piazza we wanted to create an urban room. The glass-and-steel structure opens it up to the outside. It gives one the sense of an institution that reaches out to people. Inside, the atmosphere is calm, befitting a library, but it is enough to look up, and outside you can see Manhattan rushing by with its usual frenzy.

So then the Morgan is just fine? No regrets for the Surveyor? What would he change today? If it is true that our reach always exceeds our grasp, there must be something. This would be the first time that he succeeded in realizing exactly what he had in mind.

Hmph. Too bad about that elevator in the middle, going up and down, as if this were a big hotel. It's a little dull.

I was sure something was off again. Loath though he is to admit it, a rift had opened up inside him, a place for me to delve into perhaps. Maybe this downtime has prompted him to question himself, maybe his lower-back pain has made him more susceptible. My father has lowered his guard. I take a crack: So. You've made mistakes too?

Do you mean in life or in architecture? In either case, yes, I have. I'm definitely not telling you about the mistakes I've made in my life. As for architecture, nothing comes to mind at the moment.

The rain stops. The pier is full of puddles that adults avoid and kids hunt for. There is still a sheen draped over the city, but it will evaporate soon.

More than anything there remains the tart, poignant, after-rain scent. Scientists say the smell is caused by a chemical reaction, a mix of grass, cement, dirt, living beings, and the sea. They call it petrichor.

In the meantime, my father had mulled things over. He always answers after a lag.

Sure, there are all the things that didn't turn out well, and there are mistakes. The problem is that by the time you realize your mistakes, it's too late. In architecture, once something's done it's done.

The Potsdamer Platz in Berlin, for example, is too monotonous a design. It fails to surprise.

In Los Angeles, at the County Museum, I'm unsatisfied with the BCAM (Broad Contemporary Art Museum). I got carried away oversimplifying the volume. The original design was much more interesting. It is too boxy, too bulky, has lost all its articulation. It should have levitated and been in better dialogue with the street. Instead it sits there, graceless. The building faces Miracle Mile, but your gaze doesn't manage to take in all that lies beyond it. It lacks transparency. But it is no one's fault but mine.

Architecture is enriched by all that is beautiful, sane, and authentic, from innovation to nature to the needs of people. Unfortunately it is also conditioned by thousands of things that endanger it: power, money, urgency. And if you let yourself be persuaded by something that dilutes the original idea, you are the one ultimately at fault.

Owing to changes, the Entrance Pavilion at LACMA (the Los Angeles County Museum of Art) is as dull as a gas station.

In Lyon, the Cité Internationale is too opaque. It sits heavily on the ground, and the corridor is frequently broken up; a hotel and the convention hall block your passage, and you cannot walk the length of it.

In Paris, the Atelier Brancusi next to Beaubourg lacks tension.

And in London, St. Giles doesn't manage to bring the square to life.

There are other things, I'm sure.

But you do not live for what you have done in the past, whether you regret those things or take satisfaction in them. You live for what you have yet to do and what you haven't even begun to imagine.

Let's change the subject.

9

THE PRAIRIES OF THE WHITNEY

D ay 128 of the periplus undertaken by Carlo Piano (the present author) and his father Renzo, the Explorer. From the deck of the *Magnaghi*, you can see more than the jagged forest of glass and steel. To the south, near Chelsea, stands a building that looks like a ship in dry dock, blue as the open sea beyond the Hudson. I wonder if this part of the river is freshwater or saltwater. No one on board has ever tasted it.

Not the boatswain busy re-splicing rope nor the deck officer, sub-lieutenant Valente, recording the pantry supplies in the ship's log. They will serve us on our return voyage to Europe. He is also taking down the names of those getting on and off the ship, and the times they get on and off, in the left column. The log tells the story of our voyage: our route, our sightings, our stops, the money spent, the accidents, our average speed, which sailors have taken sick, what repairs have been performed by Chief Engineer Sergio Cozzani. Cozzani is from Manarola, a tiny town on the cliffs overlooking the Ligurian Sea near La Spezia, a place as rugged as the engineer himself.

The salinity of the Hudson remains a mystery. Maybe because outlets are by their nature ambiguous. Is it the river that penetrates the sea? Or does the sea creep into the earth?

In my opinion it's a toss-up, since the waters mix. Traveling out to sea, the freshwater dissolves into the salt, thereby creating a hazy area where freshwater fish swim alongside saltwater fish, all passionately together—perch and grouper, catfish and cod.

The ship in dry dock that we look out on from the forecastle has a name: the Whitney Museum of American Art. Coordinates: 40°44'22" North, 74°0'32" West. Or simply 99 Gansevoort Street.

I was at the construction site of the Morgan Library when they called me. Leonard Lauder, then president of the board of the Whitney, was looking for me. He wanted to get together for a chat.

It was supposed to be informal. Instead, when I arrived at the museum on Madison Avenue the next day, the entire management committee was there, arrayed before me. Though it wasn't the first time I'd been ambushed, it took me by surprise.

I accept the fact that I have to participate in competitions, but it is common knowledge I don't much care for them. They easily develop into beauty pageants. And then, I admit, I don't like working on a project, getting swept up in it, maybe even falling in love with an idea, only to have it go up in smoke. You have to come up with your own design and if you don't win the competition, the design turns into a regret.

Anyway, the story of the Whitney is fascinating but complicated.

As I understand it, the adventure of this museum was plagued by second thoughts and hard-fought decisions. Various architects had already grappled with designing the new site, and nothing had ever turned out right.

The Whitney dates way back, to the time Gertrude Vanderbilt Whitney founded an artists' club in 1914. Membership cost a dollar, I believe. The club was in Greenwich Village, close to where the new Whitney would return one hundred years later.

See for yourself. It looks a bit like a retired ship, grounded for careening. One side looks out onto the water, the other the city. The eastern side is in dialogue with New York, while the Western side faces immense sunsets, the sea, the open prairies of the Far West—the rest of the world. The place has that magic.

Its history mirrors the history of American art. It is not rooted in the distant past. There are no Della Francescas or Giottos or Caravaggios. For historical reasons, there couldn't have been. Art history, in Gertrude's time, was embodied by flesh-and-blood people, not studied in books.

The artists Whitney assembled were often broke. She collected their paintings and sculptures and promoted their work. She created a sort of coterie for talented artists to congregate and converse.

In 1928, when the director of the Metropolitan Museum turned down her donation of the five hundred paintings in her gallery, she decided to open an independent museum in the Village. It was not until many years after her death, in the mid 1960s, that the museum moved uptown, for reasons of space. The Upper East Side was a residential neighborhood and much more bourgeois, a far cry from the scene in the Village, which was a hotbed of avant-garde movements.

But the ordeal of the Whitney had only just begun. In a few years' time the new building, designed by Marcel Breuer, ran out of room to store the mountain of artwork they had. We're talking about art, American art, that is fed by a living culture in a vast, constantly changing country.

The initial five hundred works had turned into more than twenty thousand, by three thousand different artists. The museum responded by moving some of its business to nearby buildings. It was a painful and arduous decision. In fact, one of the goals of the new design was to reunite the exhibition spaces with the offices of the curators and conservators.

By the time they contacted me, they had been trying to expand the Breuer, without success, for almost twenty years.

Archi-mania

What kept them from succeeding? I ask the Old Man, who has now sat back down on his canvas chair in the middle of the quarterdeck. He places a plaid blanket over his lap, a detail he'd rather I keep off the record.

They tried several times. Michael Graves did the first design in 1985, and it was blocked by residents in the neighborhood. Then Rem Koolhas tried, but again nothing came of it. Why I'm not sure.

I know that my father struggled a lot, too. In the end, after much brooding, they changed the location. The birth of the new Whitney was complicated.

Yes, it was a long process marked by doubts and various missteps that may have been necessary and inevitable. We immediately thought of expanding there, on the corner of Madison and 75th, demolishing the next-door brownstone.

Then we changed our mind. You know, I have never liked demolition. I always loved the building that Breuer built for the Whitney, but the truth is that the Whitney was no longer in the right location. The place where we erected the new site represents, in some way, a return to its true environment.

The basic idea was to raise the building, free up the ground floor, bring the street inside the museum, and create a piazza that opened up to the city.

The piazza, once again the piazza for people to gather, to linger in . . .

Again, naturally. I may be fixated and repetitive, but coherence is absolutely necessary on both a professional and cultural level. Without a healthy stubbornness you will never arrive at the heart of things.

But let's get back to the Meatpacking District. Rather than gobble up the ground floor, the museum needed to let the city in. I always tell the young people who come to our building workshop to pay careful attention to how you begin a project.

I start with the piazza, always. Empty space comes before crowded space, just as the piazza waits to fill with people. All cities have such spaces: it is not a building but a space that represents—that is the very essence of—a city.

The square is the great urban and political invention of the classic world. The new site of Columbia University grew up around a square, as did the Centre Pompidou and the old port in Genoa, wedged between the city of stone and the watery gulf. There is the agora at the Niarchos Foundation in Athens enclosed by the National Opera and the National Library. In the Auditorium in Rome there is the cavea, just as there once were in the amphitheaters of ancient Rome.

In the case of the Whitney it is more like a square, which lies half underneath and half outside the museum. We carved it out by raising the edifice off the ground and cutting its volume diagonally so as to let the light fall on it.

Once again the street, the city conveying its energy indoors, bringing life to the permeable building. The idea is always the same, and he justifies himself by calling it stubborness.

Of course I repeat it, because that is how it is: the relationship between your building and the city is fundamental for it to function. It is all of a piece, made up of empty spaces and spaces filled with sounds, odors, the rhythms of life, and states of mind.

That is why an architect cannot be oblivious to the cities in which he works, cannot be a tourist. He must understand them, walk them, listen to them, feel they are his own. In short, adopt them.

Sure, there are cities in which you feel a bit lost. Lost among their signs, language, writing and noise. But luckily all cities, and the art of coexistence, share certain universal values.

That is how you come to feel, by some miracle, like a Berliner in Berlin, an Athenian in Athens, a New Yorker in New York.

Straulino and the Wind

Hence the Whitney was not built on the Upper East Side.

Just as, at sea, you occasionally have to alter your course to avoid a storm. The boatswain knows every sheltering place. He chooses them based on the direction of the currents and winds. He grew up on the water and knows how to read the warning signs.

Whenever there's talk of wind, my father brings up the story of Agostino Straulino, the sailboat racer who learned to flirt with the breeze when just a kid. Every day Straulino had to take a boat from Lussino, the island in Croatia where he was born, to get to school. He traveled by sailboat.

Straulino always won when we raced, because he could conjure the wind. He used to say that he and the wind knew one another from the day he was born. Obviously he didn't conjure it; no one can do that. But Straulino knew the wind well, knew where it was, chased it down and found it every time. There's a life lesson in that.

And where was the wind for the Whitney, I ask the Old Man, who had raced Straulino in vain. What was the right course to follow?

Not the initial one. We worked on the first design on Madison Avenue for roughly two years. But for many reasons it turned out to be the wrong choice. Probably for the same reasons that previous attempts had failed.

The most significant being the impossibility of gathering all the departments into one new building. For what it would yield, that solution took too great an effort and incurred too great a cost. Even in the throes of passion you need a clear head.

Don't rush to fall in love with a solution, otherwise you'll never turn back.

So you regretted it and decided to move the site, to go back to the origins of the club. The Whitney is a museum dedicated to American art; its roots in American culture run deep. Maybe returning to the place where it began was, even symbolically, the right solution.

I don't regret the idea.

Actually, the idea of an open and tolerant museum remained; it just traveled the length of Manhattan and was used in the final design on the other end of the city. We couldn't stay on the Upper East Side, and moving south was a way to return the museum to its roots, to bring it back home.

B-flat Trumpet

They chose an area I know, one I'd passed through many times, a neighborhood that used to be home to slaughterhouses: the Meatpacking District. The slaughterhouses have now been replaced by boutiques, which is not necessarily a bad thing. Cities change. It still has an industrial vibe, despite the shop windows, the shopping, etc.

✔ Herman Melville once lived there, and it was there that he decided to set sail for Liverpool as a cabin boy. They say that he began to develop the idea for *Moby-Dick* on that crossing. The novel is my father's favorite, I think. Every ten years he rereads it. It takes him a while because he's a slow reader. Very slow, but he reads.

I reread it all the time. Because I fell in love with it when I first read it, at eighteen. Because *Moby-Dick* is a universal book, which helps you understand the earth and the vastness of the sea.

In my opinion, there is something about the mad figure of Captain Ahab that he finds attractive—Ahab's courage, perhaps, his struggle, his torment. Or maybe he's intrigued by Ahab's stubbornness. The same doggedness is compelling my father to look for Atlantis and makes him certain—reason be damned—that the island must exist.

What do I have to do with Ahab? What animates Ahab is his thirst for revenge. It is less about persistence than his obsession with the white whale.

He equips the *Pequod* for the sole purpose of hunting it, deceiving his crew. The stubbornness I'm talking about is another thing entirely, it drives you to dig deeper and constantly question whether you are right or not. You have to try to understand things, and humility helps, but if you aren't as stubborn as a mule you won't succeed in defending your work.

It all begins when you're little. At least it did for me.

In my childhood I gave vent to my stubbornness by collecting stamps, figurines, toy soldiers, and model trains and airplanes.

Children are usually stubborn. Though not necessarily attached to intelligence, stubbornness becomes a gift when it evolves into a tenacious defense of that which you hold dear. It usually develops into obstinacy before adolescence.

Later I began to turn to more stimulating things. Film, for example, was a great passion of mine. I grew up with Westerns and adventure movies.

Another passion was reading. I devoured books, in part because my mother forced me to. Then I moved on to music. Tone deaf as I was, I got it into my head that I would play the trumpet, the B-flat trumpet, by no means an easy instrument. You have to create the note by applying pressure with your lips.

But I was hopeless. So, in the end, I turned all of my attention to architecture. Sure, you change your mind, and out of curiosity try many different things.

Yet it is obstinacy that leads you to take an active role, to not merely spectate. To try.

Sandy

We are talking about the Whitney, about the museum's return downtown.

Under the directorship of Adam Weinberg, the museum board and I chose a neighborhood that was in the midst of change. One side faced the Hudson River, the other the end of the High Line, right where demolition of the elevated train was interrupted, before they decided to turn it into an urban garden. One adventure had come to a conclusion on that site, and we imagined another could begin: the adventure of the new Whitney.

I was so enthusiastic the day of the first inspection that when I saw a For Rent sign across the street, on Washington Street, I thought that we could open our New York office there. And we did. We went to visit the space the next morning and to this day we continue to work there.

Moving the museum was not the only change of plans. I know, for example, that they had originally wanted to use stone for the façade. You had to wonder why that idea was abandoned. The Constructor had used stone—reimagined stone—in many works: limestone in Valletta, Apricena stone in the Padre Pio Pilgrimage Church, stone from Patagonia for the Fondation Beyeler in Basel.

We worked a lot on the possibility of using stone, but it seemed a bit out of place in an area full of industrial buildings. So we decided to use steel instead, light blue varnished panels. The color plays off of the shimmering light of New York, the intense sunsets on the river, the clouds.

Then came the rain. A lot of rain.

"In three and a half years, Hurricane Sandy was the only mishap," the foreman told me. "It was October 29, 2012. We heard the alarm but at that point couldn't protect the construction site. The base of the lobby had been only partially installed, so the basement floor wasn't covered yet. We found ourselves in a helpless situation: the river had flooded and the winds were blowing the water toward the building, completely swamping the foundations."

The subway lines and streets ended up underwater. Half the city lost power during the blackout.

Terrible. There's always something to be learned.

After the incident we improved the building's security system to protect against similarly extraordinary events. Today, in a few hours, you can assemble a series of barriers that seal off the ground floor and prevent flooding. To defend against nature, you have to have an intimate understanding of how hostile nature can be. And never give in to fatalism. Never.

Before Sandy they had placed the entrance three meters above sea level, the highest elevation predicted for floods in the next five hundred years. But the hurricane forever shattered that benchmark.

When you create a public building, one destined for a community, you need to believe it will last a thousand years, or more.

For the Whitney, the experience of Sandy is engraved in the structures and protections that we added; it is braced for all possible tides and every potential gust of wind.

Bread and Jam

The Whitney floats on air. Even the terraces that face Chelsea look like the tiered decks of a container ship, like the ones on the river facing west.

Vessel, ocean liner, container ship: everyone can sort of see what they want.

This building was designed by the forces of necessity—by topographical, functional, and economic constraints.

But also by the force of the imagination. The two are related. Architecture is the art of giving people shelter, but it also responds to their hopes and dreams. Actually, the sociologist Paul-Henry Chombart de Lauwe believed that dreams could be more powerful than needs. Even the most modest hut is no simple roof. Buildings celebrate more than shelter.

They represent those who inhabit the place. A house expresses a desire to belong, an identity. You might say architecture tells stories. Differently from film and literature, but it does. In architecture the pragmatic world of making and the world of imagining blur. Necessity alone would design dreary buildings, yet who knows where you would be if all you had was desire. Desires are like fantasies: fine in moderation. Or like jam: better by the spoonful, and better still if spread over a hard slice of bread.

I know where he had picked up that last image.

In a television interview, a journalist once asked Calvino: "Will humanity still be capable of fantasy in the next millennium?"

Calvino shook his head before answering: "I am rather skeptical of that creative imperative. I believe that, firstly, what is needed is a foundation of accuracy, method, pragmatism, and a sense of reality."

Crossing his legs (a tic of his), he continued, "Only a certain prosaic solidity can give birth to creativity. Fantasy is like jam; you have to spread it on a solid slice of bread. If not, it remains a shapeless thing, like jam, out of which you can't make anything."

Also attending the opening of the Whitney was then first lady Michelle Obama, who stopped to admire Alexander Calder's *Circus* and Andy Warhol's *Green Coca-Cola Bottles*, and afterward climbed the stairs up to the four terraces. The climb was slow, since the steps impede one from moving fast. She liked that sense of delay, and the public square, which is the domain of slowness. Michelle had appreciated the pleasures of the flâneur.

I like it too, the idea of a museum being a welcoming public square, a space where speed gives way to slowness.

Columbia University—we'll visit later—is a space of scientific exploration that operates under the belief that globalization can produce a better world. Here at the Whitney there is an idea of

American art as free from the burden of tradition. My generation grew up thinking of America as the land of freedom.

I used to love to listen to Fernanda Pivano talk about literature, about Steinbeck, Hemingway, Kerouac and others. To discover America meant to explore its open spaces and sweeping prairies—whether real or imagined.

When you come from a place like Europe, a place with cultural roots that run deep, there is a danger of remaining stuck in the splendors of the past. Maybe we need to know how to pull back and get some distance.

But distance serves another more practical need: to see better. That's what the maestros of the mosaics in Ravenna did. They had to be quite close to the mosaic to concentrate on each tessera. Then, every once and a while, they would pull back to look at the whole work and see what they were doing.

Film, too, with its closeups and wide angles, constantly shuttles between fragment and whole. I do the same when I travel: I pull back to better understand the proportions of things.

As I was saying, my generation grew up convinced that American art was a breath of fresh air: Hopper, Lichtenstein, Rauschenberg, Warhol, John Cage, Merce Cunningham. American art is somehow bound up with rebellion, with freedom from the chains of the past. And that building interprets it for what it is: free, surprising, often discordant; even, when it serves, formless.

Apocalypse in the Vatican

Free, surprising . . . He began in Paris with Rogers, building a museum as if it were a manufacturing plant. He redid it here in the Meatpacking District. He is doing it now by converting a power station in Moscow. Two hectares of urban decay, just behind the Kremlin, are being transformed into a cultural and artistic hub. I hear a faint echo of the museum/factory—utopian ideal or the trivialization of the idea of a museum?

Maybe. But I never cared much for the idea of a museum as a sanctuary. I always regarded it with a certain suspicion.

The first half of the 1960s in Milan saw the first university occupations.

By day I worked at Albini's studio and at night I occupied the university.

Bertolt Brecht's *Threepenny Opera* was playing at the theater, John Cassavetes' experiments at the cinema. Art, all art, was a means of scrutinizing the future and believing in a better world. And all that passion wasn't found in the museums but in the streets, the squares, the theaters.

And when Richard and I entered the Pompidou competition in Paris, those feelings weighed on us.

Imagine how offended we were by the snide description of the Pompidou as a cultural refinery or manufacturing plant.

Speaking of Yankee art, when my father was designing the church of Padre Pio, Rauschenberg was supposed to depict a scene of the Apocalypse on the large window facing the church porch. But he never did. It's a story of stinging defeat. Something didn't sit right with the Vatican commission appointed to approve the fresco.

I was there that day in the Palazzo with Rauschenberg, who showed up carrying an enormous roll under his arm. My father loaned me a jacket; the arms were too long, and it was tight in the shoulders. They received us in a hall in the middle of which was a rectangular mahogany table. The kind you might find in a sacristy, only five times larger. To get to the room we had to climb a staircase. Rauschenberg wheezed; he wasn't a kid anymore.

I was working for a newspaper at the time and was supposed to interview him. We had already agreed to it, and I had even provided him a few questions in advance. But the meeting at the Vatican was tense. As soon as I saw the sketch I knew why: Rauschenberg had depicted God in the form of a satellite dish. The Vatican commission was not amused. They saw in it the seeds of heresy. They argued over the colorful sketch for a long time, in terms hardly clerical.

On our way out, Rauschenberg's tread was heavy, solemn. His footsteps echoed in the empty halls of the Holy See, halls as wide as alleyways. Portraits of popes hanging on the walls glared down at us. They seemed to be reprimanding us for that satellite God. The vaulted ceiling was frescoed with scenes from the Old Testament. Any minute now, I thought, a lightning bolt is going to incinerate all three of us.

Sure, I remember. It still stings.

The Apocalypse as a happy moment for humanity and God an antenna, in Rauschenberg's words. The embarrassed silences of the prelates. Me trying to mitigate the situation using the old lost-in-translation trick. Rauschenberg was angry. I can still hear the reports of his footsteps. He never wanted to speak to me again.

10.
DESPERATELY SEEKING RENZO

I don't see him anymore. As we were heading back up the High Line toward the heart of Manhattan, I lost sight of my father. Or maybe he lost me.

An Italian tourist and his girlfriend stopped me to ask for directions. They held a map marked with places to visit, the same places the whole world has seen on TV. It is as if, for us foreigners, whose eyes have been saturated with its image, the city were one long bout of déjà vu. Having hung back with them, I lost the Explorer. But I have an excuse: the elevated park is a leisurely walkway. Only the old tracks, visible here and there, recall the rush of the past, a time when trains went whistling by. In the absence of their din, which once upon a time disturbed sleep and marked time, the voice of New York had changed. I was distracted momentarily, and he disappeared into the shrubs and flowers. Even now, at the end of January, marigold, heather, and cyclamens bloom, indifferent to the cold.

Maybe he was swept up in the magic of that airborne promenade, floating ten meters above ground. Not high enough to make you forget you're still in the city. The throbs of jackhammers, however muffled, reach us. The elevated walkway is an unusual observation deck: you can see straight into the windows of the buildings. Nothing remains private. A couple arguing on a balcony, a work meeting, a man pointing to numbers on a chalkboard, a woman cradling her little son, two kids biting into a hot dog. Some houses, however, keep their secrets hidden behind blinds.

I can't find my father. He isn't here. Calling is pointless, he'd never pick up. My best option is to go to the Columbia construction site in Manhattanville, in West Harlem, above 125th. I hope to find him there.

Canal Street

At the Canal Street Station I bump into the boatswain circling New York in a daze. In a city of nearly nine million inhabitants, I had to run into Giobatta of all people. He's more comfortable steering through breakers than the rivers of people flowing through the streets, his confidence with a windlass equal to his bewilderment at the neon signs of New York.

I invite him to come see the (partially complete) birth of Columbia's campus, or rather, Columbia University in the City of New York.

The official name is not insignificant; it attests to its being an urban university, firmly embedded in the city, unlike many other eminent universities that lie in the mildly tedious quiet of the countryside. Giobatta peppers me with questions about the project. I have to tell him something. I'll figure it out. When we meet my father again, he'll be able to talk specifics. What I do know is that the original campus building was designed by McKim, the same architect who designed the Morgan. The boatswain presses me for details. "Is it a library? I thought we were going to a university?" It's my fault for creating confusion and leading him astray.

Let's start over. When it was founded, Columbia was a safe space, closed off to the city around it. Culture and knowledge at the turn of the twentieth century were treated like a gated community. Universities were modeled on forts, and perhaps at the time it was necessary for their safety. But above all they championed the idea of a serious, inviolable place reserved for a select few. Even their neoclassical style harkened back to the solemnity of European culture.

Theodore Roosevelt and Barack Obama studied at Columbia, and the physicist Enrico Fermi taught there. More than one hundred Nobel Prizes have been conferred on students, researchers, and professors from the university.

"Fermi," asks the boatswain, "the nuclear reactor guy?"

The same. One of the many minds who left Italy and came to America.

But the story of Columbia is not studded with trophies only. Even the most eminent institutions sometimes bump up against societal change and contradictions. It suffered growing pains, some logistical. It outgrew the hill in Morningside and was therefore expanded, in spurts, one piece at a time. It encroached on the neighborhood, fueling tensions among the residents.

In 1968 it was accused of racial discrimination. Its construction of a park gym sparked urban warfare. There were protests, occupations, and arrests; kids were clubbed by the police. The university had a strained, love–hate relationship with its neighboring city.

Giobatta the Humanist

Meanwhile, inside the rattling subway car, entertained by acrobats twirling in the aisle, we reach the 116th stop. At stations like this, the racket of the train is remarkable: a rumble that keeps churning, interrupted only by the more deafening screech of the brakes. Luckily, by the exit, an a cappella group is singing Carl Orff's "Carmina Burana" and collecting donations for a "Singing under the Streets" initiative. A Chinese man plays the violin, Mozart most likely.

Legend has it that a shadow community lives underneath

the city, in the nooks and crannies of the defunct tunnels. The destitute, the insane, and the crack-addled have taken shelter underground, transforming the tunnels into campsites. Some people swear they have seen them going in and out of the grates in the early morning hours, while Manhattan is still sleeping. But I have my doubts.

When Lee Bollinger became the president of Columbia in 2002, he contacted my father almost immediately. I believe he was looking for a humanist eye, hoping to yoke the growth of the university to the growth of the neighborhood, and mindful, perhaps, of past mistakes. This wasn't just any place. It was Harlem. The cradle of street culture.

Here, everything takes place on the street: food, music, crafts, art, sports. Even business is conducted on the street. Vendors own the sidewalks. They sell food, clothes, books, even jewelry. They wheel carts and fridges out onto the street, carry bags and crates over their shoulders. They shuttle in and out of La Marqueta, the neighborhood marketplace on Park Avenue. Bodegas selling tropical fruit sit next to stalls frying hamburgers and kebabs. Pharmacies stand shoulder to shoulder with botanicas that peddle miracle medicinal herbs and religious objects. The kind used by Santerians, voodoo priests.

The boatswain looks puzzled as he struggles to light his cigarette in the wind. Something has escaped him, a subject not covered at the Maddalena Noncommissioned Officer Academy. "What do you mean 'humanist'?" he asks. I try to answer. It's an uncommon word, one hardly spoken anymore.

What is a humanist? Essentially, a humanist is someone who knows how to marry, say, the world of science with that of art, memory with invention. Leon Battista Alberti was an architect, but he also wrote about childhood education and drew up codices about cryptography. According to my father, being Italian helps you grasp the larger story, gives you the perspective you need to see the bigger picture.

He says that he feels like a humanist, even if he doesn't have a literary or artistic background. He said it himself: at school he was a dunce. When he was in third grade a priest swore on the cross that little Renzo was a lost cause. My grandmother Rosa took him to a psychologist, who diagnosed him as a child of normal intelligence. He couldn't study and got distracted in class, but he was not a fool.

I remember once, many years ago, an exhibit for my father at Palazzo Tursi in Genoa. One of the visitors was his old art history teacher, then retired, who had come to have a look at her former student's works.

He greeted her. "Good day, Miss," he said. "Remember me?"

The teacher answered that, yes, of course she remembered him.

"You must have," he added. "You always made me repeat exams in September . . ."

She didn't argue. Instead she put an end to the conversation. "And don't you see how well it served you?"

The boatswain looks increasingly perplexed.

Street Life

Bollinger had to discuss the project with the Harlem community, as is customary. The new Columbia could not impose its will from on high, especially in a neighborhood where kids play and old people perch on stoops. A vantage point for overseeing the city, as well as a place to flirt and who knows what else. The language of the stoops is a mix of English and Caribbean Spanish, or African-American jive. In the span of a block you come across the adventure of the world.

Baccan Pasculli says that, after weathering enough months at sea together, a good crew creates its own language. A language neither Italian nor Sardinian nor Genoese nor Sicilian. The same happens in Harlem.

This is where kids began to dance to the beat of hip hop, and rappers like Puff Daddy, Freekey Zekey, and Charles Hamilton faced off amid the rusty fire escapes. Harlem has always been the crucible of Black America. Malcolm X was headquartered at the Hotel Theresa and assassinated at a rally in the Audubon Ballroom. All of that took place in a radius of four blocks, the same streets where *West Side Story* is set. Today Hispanic Americans make up one half of the ethnic mix, African Americans and whites the other half. Someone once said that the city's splendor is encapsulated in its variety.

So, from 2003 to 2008, he spoke with the people and to the people about the project. Listening is a complex art: the greatest difficulty is that often the voices with the most interesting things to say are the softest and most discreet. They don't rant and rave, and they don't try to dictate to others.

But the point of listening is not to dazzle or convince. "No," the Old Man always says, "you have to listen to understand. To understand!" Some people spend their lives trying to persuade others what they think when they'd be better spent looking for good ideas. Especially given the social risk of architecture: a bad book can be put down, bad music switched off, but a big ugly building must be endured.

The boatswain is growing increasingly confused. I wonder if I haven't been clear enough. Unsure, I quote my missing traveling companion: "In the 1800s the university was an exclusive system to be protected. Today the opposite is true. The operation is inclusive. The university must be a place of integration, with no more barriers and fences sealing it off from the outside world. In the past academies were self-referential. By seeking vitality through exchange, they are becoming open places where you can breathe in the city on every corner."

Traditionally, at the intersection of Lenox and 125th Street here in Harlem, anyone who wanted to could hold a rally. They called it "the university on the corner."

Cotton Club

A single underground network, where the energy systems are, connects the entire campus. On the transparent ground floor are the businesses and centers that invite the public in, that share the space with Harlem. The top floors are reserved for classes and research. As we nose around the construction site, a vivid flow of people streams toward us on the street. It's like swimming in a pastiche of faces and sounds. The pounding of drills, the clunk of cars passing over steel road plates, laughter, the wail of firetrucks, the trash-talk of basketball players.

Some claim that New Yorkers walk faster, talk faster, and think faster than others. There must be a molecule in the air that makes sleep superfluous. Perhaps that's most true of Harlem, where the nightlife explodes with jazz. Orchestras once got their start in glorified basement venues, Duke Ellington played at the Cotton Club, and Ella Fitzgerald and James Brown sang at the Apollo Theater.

Giobatta glances at his watch, an old Bulova corroded by the salt air. He has to be back on board to relieve his helmsmen. There is a shift schedule, and it must be respected, and it's Giobatta's turn to take the "Diana shift," from three to seven in the morning, so-called because Diana is the goddess of the moon.

Still no trace of my father. Where could he have gone? Off to size something up? He has taken my measurements since I was in the cradle, further back than I can remember. And every time he sees my sister, he measures her with his yellow roll-up tape, even if she stopped growing a long time ago. He measures all his children all the time. My nose has been the object of keen interest. He tries to put a number on everything, not just the visible world, but invisible forces too. On the rare occasion Milly drags him to church, he taps his finger to calculate the organ's reverb.

He organizes competitions with his friends, engineers mostly, as he once did with Peter Rice. Whoever comes closest to guessing a distance, a width, a circumference, a weight, or the light intensity, wins. The margin of error hovers around ten percent. Most recently, two days ago in the port, he calculated that a seagull with its wings extended one meter flies at the speed of nearly ten meters per second.

The *nostrummu* is itching to go, time is running out, and the *Magnaghi* is a long way away. "What is it they do in these hangars?" he asks. "Hangar" might not be the most appropriate word for these buildings.

There is the Zuckerman Institute, directed by Nobel Laureates Eric Kandel and Richard Axel, where they study the brain. Not only on a psychological level. They explore, via observation, the structure of the brain. Nine hundred researchers are at work searching for a cure for degenerative brain disorders, primarily Alzheimer's, Parkinson's, and autism. On average the specialists are under thirty years old, because for a long-term project lasting half a century, it is essential to have young people who will still be alive when the job is completed.

There is beauty in all of this, the beauty of knowledge and scientific inquiry. To discover, to understand, to invent. Like Archimedes crying out, "Eureka!" upon stepping into a bathtub and realizing that the volume of water displaced was equal to the volume of the part of his body submerged. Beauty is not only an aesthetic but a generative force for progress.

That is what the poet and president of Senegal, Léopold Senghor, with whom my father had collaborated, sought to recapture. He used to say that in African languages the word for "beautiful" is the same word for "good"; no distinction is made between the two. The same goes for Greece and all the cultures lapped by the Mediterranean. We'll have to talk about it when I find my father again. But beauty is also an unattainable idea, the dream of perfection that will never be achieved. A little like our Atlantis.

Columbia is also home to the Lenfest Center for the Arts, the University Forum, and the Global Center to address issues of globalization: energy, clean water, climate change.

My phone rings. It's my father. He had gone wandering around Harlem. Then he heard a song, gospel music emanating from the First Corinthian Baptist Church, and had stopped to listen, or perhaps to calculate the pitch and timber of the sound. Like the boatswain, he's now in a hurry. "I'm back on the *Magnaghi*. Get down here. We have to talk about peripheries." So, we rush back on board without a second thought.

11.
The City of the Future

My father is waiting for us on the bridge. "Where did you go, senator?" asks the boatswain. But he doesn't wait for a reply. He has to relieve the watch, there are routine inspections to be made. He had enumerated them for me, but there are so many I struggle to remember them.

Ahead of us is our latest sally out to sea, from New York to London. This time we'll be braving the Atlantic, the most notorious of all the oceans, especially when sailing east, subject of the most terrifying stories, stories of hundred-foot waves that mount all of a sudden and snap oil tankers in two, like sticks. According to researchers, these rogue waves form in one of two ways. First, when sets of different waves combine, the waves can cancel each other out, but sometimes they merge to form monster waves. Second, when strong currents run counter to the direction of the waves, the collision produces waves much larger than the original sets.

But the perils of the Atlantic don't end there. From May to September there is fog, from April to December hurricanes. During the hurricane season, storms are whipped up by south-westerly winds. Our trip will take at least two weeks. That's a long time, considering that in 1993 the Italian ocean liner *Rex* crossed the Atlantic in four days and change. The captain of the *Rex*, Francesco Tarabotto, was from Lerici, the Golfo dei Poeti. His exploits are legendary on board.

The boatswain addressed my father as "*sciü* senator." He was teasing, but the truth is, a few years ago, my father was in fact appointed a senator for life, an honorific that exists only in Italy, I believe. The British have lords, but that is different. In Italy you can sit in the senate not by being elected, but by being chosen on the grounds of "social, scientific, artistic, and literary merit." Its recipients include the poet Eugenio Montale, the scientist Rita Levi-Montalcini, and the conductor Claudio Abbado, a close friend of the Old Man who was made senator at the same time as my father. Abbado had hoped to introduce music into the schools, but he passed away before he had the chance. The Quirinale called on August 2013.

I was in a taxi in New York, sitting in traffic, and they told me that the President of the Republic urgently wanted to speak with me. Giorgio Napolitano explained that he intended to appoint me and Claudio Abbado.

During that time Claudio and I spoke often.

What would I do? What would he do?

I thought of the movie *Il Postino*, in which Pablo Neruda tells the postman, "I'm a poet, and what I have to say I say in poetry."

I'm an architect. And what I have to say I say in architecture, by building.

That is how I hit upon the idea to focus on peripheries.

Mending

So, with an assist from Don Pablo Neruda, my father had his flash of insight concerning *periferie*—urban peripheries have always been his passion. For him, raised in Pegli, the center of Genoa was remote and intimidating.

When he was a student in Milan, he lived in Lambrate, one of the frontiers separating the city from the industrial area. He listened to jazz concerts at the Capolinea night club, in the Navigli district, the last stop on the 19 tram.

And he always built and worked on the edges. It was the end of the 1970s. I was still a child, but some things I recall, like hearing people argue about participation, mobile construction sites, "archidoctors," the importance of listening to one another and involving residents in design plans. To this day his most important buildings lie on these peripheries: the Paris Courthouse in the northern banlieue, the École normale supérieure in Paris-Saclay and, as we have just seen, Columbia University in Harlem.

Italy is a beautiful country, but fragile.

Its landscape is fragile, its cities are fragile, and most of all its peripheries are fragile, fragile and forgotten. But peripheries are the city of the future, where the energy is concentrated. They are full of humanity and vitality, and they abound with young people. They are factories of ambition. They are the beauty that has yet to come. The beauty of historic cities was built by our ancestors, no thanks to us. On the contrary, we can be unworthy heirs.

But what we can do is render our peripheries beautiful.

More often than not we built them poorly, carelessly, almost with disdain.

So, I thought that there was a need for a largescale operation to mend these spaces, and that would be my job as senator.

Beautiful verb, to mend: to repair, as opposed to discarding. When my father was working on the Expo in Genoa, then mayor Fulvio Cerofolini gave him just one piece of advice: "Look Piano, *chì nù se straggia nìnte.*" Nothing goes to waste here. Parsimony is a great virtue.

Of course, mending calls to mind the ancient practice of saving energy, time, means, and space.

In cities, art is what stitches together the urban fabric.

I'm talking about construction sites that do not force residents out of their homes while renovations are underway. I'm talking about unobtrusive and tolerant construction sites.

At this point in the conversation, the senator usually tells the story of the modern metropolis. To avoid any long digressions, I'll summarize: from the postwar period to the 1960s, Italian cities experienced a boom, robbing space from the countryside and neighboring towns. The many decaying *periferie* that surround us are the offspring of urban expansion during that time. In the 1980s cities stopped growing, having reached the physiological limits of growth. Then, starting in the 1990s, they began to implode and reabsorb the empty urban spaces abandoned by big industry.

Architecture is a civic art. For me, a city should be, first and foremost, a place that privileges social relations and diversity, that teaches you how to live with other people.

When the peripheries are neglected, everything falls into decline, from the surrounding landscape to human relations. We grow accustomed to ugliness.

That's unfortunate, since peripheries possess their own beauty. A beauty that emerges all of a sudden and is composed of solidarity, hospitality, friendship, nature, light, and, occasionally, vast horizons.

G124

As he prepares for our imminent departure, Giobatta eavesdrops on our conversation. Every once in a while he dispenses a pearl of wisdom: "The pessimist complains about the wind, the optimist waits for it to change, the realist adjusts his sails."

Giobatta also grew up on the outskirts, in Prà, and like my

father felt the call of the sea. He would stroll along the pebble beach where the last naval shipyards stood their ground: Mantero, Mostes, Zippo. Once upon a time those shipyards manufactured three-masted barques. He claims that the galley ships Julius Caesar used to conquer Gaul were also built in Prà. Is that true? He says he has proof but fails to provide any.

Giobatta is splicing a rope with a device called a marlinspike, forming an eye that will eventually be inserted into the mooring bitts. There are many types of splices, depending on what the line is used for: back splices, long splices, eye splices, figure-eight splices, and ring splices.

Giobatta lifts his head and asks *sciü* senator: "So, what do we have to do to keep the peripheries from going to ruin?"

First we have to stop building new ones. There are already plenty of places where the city is no longer the city and the countryside is not yet the country. We need peripheries to become cities, without their spreading like wildfire. We need to stitch them together and power them with public structures.

In particular, we need to rein in their uncontrolled growth, because, for one, it is becoming economically unstable to bring them public services. Rather than explosive, today's development must be implosive. We need to transform those spaces where there is room for growth: former industrial, military, and railroad areas.

I am talking about revitalizing the city, building over what has already been built. We don't need to tear down the peripheries. We need to change them.

It sounds paradoxical, but peripheries can be beautiful. Think of Milan's Giambellino, Catania's Librino, the area under the Viadotto dei Presidenti in Rome, or Marghera in Venice and Borgo Vittoria in Turin, which grew out of the need to house the families of Fiat workers. We've worked there, with my father and a group of young architects whom he pays with his parliamentary salary. The name, G124, has nothing to do with gatherings of powerful world leaders. It is named after the office given to them by the Senate, on the first floor of Palazzo Giustiniani, Room 24.

In the peripheries there lay a hidden harmony, however messy. In Librino the Briganti team turned a wasteland into a rugby field, attempting to rescue kids from criminal rackets by bringing them into scrums. In a parking lot in Turin, they have planted vegetables in the collective garden with the help of a parish priest, Don Angelo. In Giambellino, a wall was torn down to connect the local market to the park and thereby create a vibrant space where retired orchestra members of La Scala give music lessons and educators teach Italian to foreigners. During the summer, open-air movie theaters are mounted in the courtyards of apartment blocks: a large white sheet is used for a screen, watermelon is sliced for everyone, and people bring chairs down from their homes.

Little mends and sparks that can blaze trails and rekindle neighborhoods. You sense the pride of the people who live in them. They say their neighborhoods are not peripheries, maybe because periphery has become an ugly word, always attached to denigrating adjectives like *violent*, *remote*, *deserted*. Yet these places also have a wealth of human beauty and, as the Surveyor says, that beauty is often physical. It is as if the peripheries enjoy a beauty for which they were not built.

Maybe modesty makes it hard to invoke the word beauty. My father talks about it in a whisper. Almost every well-meaning person whispers it. Like Abbado, who wanted to use his senatorial post to bring music into the schools. Music, too, is beauty.

Claudio held one conviction: that beauty, art, culture—not the fancified academic version but that which grows out of curiosity, exploration, research—make us better people.

Have you ever noticed how art and beauty cause people's eyes to light up? He was a believer, which is why he fixated on the idea of teaching music in Italian schools. Many European schools offer music. How is it possible Italy does not? We ought to start, because beauty is an extraordinary garden, but we must enter while we're still young.

T he Atlantic had mercy on us. Our crossing was long but painless, though the ocean is never completely calm; wild currents hid underneath its wrinkled surface. The boatswain regaled us with stories about sunken ships, shipwrecks, and miraculous rescues. Some of the stories were true, like the one about Steven Callahan, a sailor who survived for four months on a raft before being picked up off the coast of Guadeloupe. Others, if you ask me, sprang from Giobatta's imagination. He talked about the mystery of the *Mary Celeste*, a Canadian-built merchant brigantine spotted between the Azores and the Portuguese coast on December 4, 1872. The ship had left New York and was bound for Genoa. On board they found everything in order: the cargo, the food supplies, water. Everything save for the seven crewmen, Captain Benjamin Briggs, his wife Sarah, and their infant daughter Matilda. What became of them was never clear, thus the *Mary Celeste* remains, among seafarers, the quintessential ghost ship.

Giobatta says that the Atlantic has always been "*grammo*." Foul. With the exception of January, the only months that the Atlantic is safe to sail are those missing the letter "r": May, June, July, and August. Yet in the middle of February our passage transpired quickly and calmly, in part because I was busy organizing the notes of our journey in search of Atlantis.

Everyone, not only my father, has personal reasons for pursuing Atlantis. They all have their reasons: the *nostrommu*,

Captain Pasculli, Chief Petty Officer Mulas, Head of the Hydrography Division Frascaro, Helmsman Giannutri, Lieutenant Tamburini, Officer Valente, Radio Operator Michele Cassano, and Savasto, the head chef, who at this moment is preparing Sunday's tiramisu.

Each of us has lost something. Someone we loved, a great opportunity, innocence, ourselves. But above all we have lost perfection, which, according to legend, once belonged to us and might still be recovered. That notion revives the hope— entertained and often dashed—that somewhere out there is a land of peace, beauty, and justice. Down there, amid the golden roofs and ivory towers, maybe we could be happy again. Down there Atlantis stirs the forgotten chords of the heart. We cling to it in order to continue this periplus, which, to be honest, I'm growing tired of.

I spoke at length with my father on the ocean, where your thoughts run free. You clear your head and are prone to intro- spection. Corvo, the smallest volcano of the Azores, was now behind us, and we could make out the blurry outline of Ilha Graciosa.

You look for Atlantis. You don't find it, but you look for it any- way. There is always something not quite right about what you do, and it makes your stomach hurt. Norberto Bobbio used to say, "Many times have I arrived at the threshold of the temple, but never have I entered."

No one arrives at the temple of absolute truth, perfect har- mony, universal wisdom, and unattainable beauty. There is a gulf between what you imagine and what you build with your hands, whether you are an architect, a writer, or a musician.

Faced with certain tasks, you always worry that you are not up to it, that you remain on the surface, that you cannot go deep enough.

Cavafy warns: "Guard, O my soul, against pomp and glory.

And if you cannot curb your ambitions, at least pursue them hesitantly, cautiously."[10]

Are we doomed to powerlessness and ineptitude?

I don't know, but we often dwell in the comedy of knowledge—or lack thereof. We hover over the surface of things, pretending we know, hoping we know, but in reality we don't. It is a farce we stage for ourselves, the tragedy of our limitations. Then again, it also frees us to carry on searching. You look for Atlantis in vain. But still you look for it, and go on looking.

Southwark

We have now reached the other side of the Atlantic and are facing the Thames Estuary. We passed Grays in a downpour that made our raincoats useless. This place is crisscrossed by oil tankers, container ships, and ferries that appear like bright dots on the radar.

We can follow the river as far as London Bridge, then we have to stop. The *Magnaghi* can go no farther because it cannot pass under the bridge.

For the same reason, merchant vessels have long dropped anchor in the middle of the Thames, entrusting their cargo and drainage to a fleet of barges. In fact, these waters were once teeming with buccaneers and plunderers. Pilfering ships used to be a lucrative enterprise. The biggest targets were large ships arriving from the West Indies, loaded with tobacco, coffee, ginger, and cocoa. Piracy is still, in a way, honored by the presence of the *Golden Hind*. Docked at St. Mary Overie, the

---

[10] "The Ides of March" in *Collected Poems* Revised Edition, translated by Edmund Keeley and Philip Sherrard, edited by George Savidis (Princeton University Press). Translation copyright © 1975, 1992 by Edmund Keeley and Philip Sherrard.

ship is a replica of the galleon manned by the corsair, explorer, and politician, Francis Drake.

Our course is set for Southwark, the oldest borough in London lying just beneath the Shard, which from offshore looks like a lighthouse: to get your bearings all you need to do is look up. To sailors the Shard represents a major landmark, a point of reference that they can discern from far away. Once you identify its position, you can determine where you are, so Petty Officer Giannutri told me.

The neighborhood of Southwark used to have a rotten reputation for being poor, dirty, and criminal. Once the domain of brothels, seedy pubs, and arenas where people placed bets on bearbaiting, Southwark was home to poor longshoremen, poor hucksters, poor weavers, poor prostitutes, streetfighters, and petty thieves—also dirt poor. Still standing is a wall of the Marshalsea prison described in the novels of Charles Dickens. Dickens' father was held there for a debt of forty pounds and ten shillings, and the future writer, twelve at the time, was forced to work in a shoe polish factory. This is the same neighborhood where Jack the Ripper, veiled by the fog of Victorian London, sow panic.

Boatswain Giobatta informs us that all the brothels have moved to Soho. Thanks for sharing, I want to say.

Nearby, a graveyard for unnamed prostitutes, the Cross Bones, still sits at the end of a cul-de-sac. Where now there is a bus depot, at least fifteen thousand women, including the so-called Winchester Geese, are buried. In a shady commingling of the sacred and profane, the women were licensed to practice their trade by the bishop of Winchester.

London Calling

Before the Shard emerged on the skyline, Southwark was

already in the midst of being revitalized, no longer the sprawl of defunct factories, docks, and railroads—what the English call brownfields. Shakespeare's Globe had been restored and the Bankside Power Station transformed into the seat of the Tate Modern.

The waters of the Thames had been brought back to life, the same waters now encircling us as the crew of the *Magnaghi* lowers the lifeboats which will ferry us to shore. In 1957 the river was declared biologically dead. It did not have enough oxygen to sustain life. Now, though hardly clear, the Thames has been resuscitated: salmon and sole swim at the mouth of the river, and you can spot seals, porpoises, and even, occasionally, whales and dolphins. Thanks are due, in part, to Ken Livingstone, the city's mayor for eight years who intensified efforts to clean up and repopulate the river.

Livingstone was governing Britain's capital when talks about the Shard began. My father was already familiar with London, having come here with his children to live and work before the Pompidou adventure. Back then, skirts kept getting shorter and hair kept getting longer. It was only a matter of time before he would return to London to design a building.

I couldn't wait. I had always wanted to erect a building on the Thames.

Whether I willed it into being or it was just my lucky stars, I can't say, but it came to pass.

A building like the Shard doesn't get made unless the planets and moons are aligned.

In Livingstone we had a visionary mayor and in Irvine Sellar a determined client.

It looks as though the top of the tower, where the peak fades into the clouds, was never completed. Passersby tend to wonder, "When are they going to finish it?" You can't blame them. For one, the original plan for the top had been different: the building was supposed to have reached 400 meters, but work stopped well short of that.

We had in mind crystal shards that tapered higher up. That dematerialization effect is the result of the angle at which they climb, so that they mirror the weather and reflect the light. The building is coming up for air.

But you're right, the initial plan was different. The building was supposed to be taller, but it was located on the City Airport's flight path. Aviation told us the building could not exceed 315 meters, otherwise it would disrupt flights. But we kept a theoretical point of 400 meters, at which, if they kept going up, the sides of the building would come together.

So the shards extend toward a point they will never reach, because the building breaks off. The peak is the product of an unfulfilled dream. It looks unfinished because it is.

Not everyone cares for it. Some criticize the way the building splinters apart. They say that the building is too tall for such playfulness. One English journalist went so far as to write that the Shard did more damage to London than the Luftwaffe.

Prince Charles compared it to a saltshaker. Supposedly, on the day of the historic regatta to honor the Queen's Jubilee, as the royal barge was sailing past the skyscraper, he turned to look away. Truth or legend?

I know the Prince. He isn't mistaken when he says that modernity has erected a lot of monstrosities, yet you could say the same about earlier generations, which produced many disasters of their own. But that is no reason to stop building things that embody the present. Even St. Paul's Cathedral was criticized at the time of its construction.

What for us are classics were once contemporary and innovative. We mustn't forget that.

Without Livingstone and Sellar, the Shard may never have been built. The mayor was tasked with proving that the city could be densified without increasing traffic. He introduced a congestion charge, a toll for driving in the city center that would reduce traffic by thirty percent. He promoted the idea of a green belt, where the woodland around London marks the border with the countryside. He understood that a building like the Shard would bring energy to the other side of the Thames. Opposite is the City, the largest financial hub in Europe, where three hundred thousand people work and a mere eight thousand people live. On weekends its streets are deserted.

Southwark hasn't fallen victim to the same trap; it is a hodgepodge of businesses. Hence the Shard is a hodgepodge— of offices, restaurants, hotels, shops, apartments, and terraces. From its observatory, The View, you can look down on London, like a bird.

Yes, the Shard is a small upright city, a building that never sleeps. The problem with towers is that they often symbolize a remote, sealed-off form of power. At six in the evening towers empty out and their gates are shut. Towers also tend to serve a single function. Usually they are nothing but offices.

We wanted the Shard to be multifunctional, to gather many businesses under the same roof.

We did not want to follow the bad example set by the City, which is abandoned outside business hours.

Are you finally satisfied, Constructor? Maybe it's just my impression, but once again he seems to harbor a regret, once again something has eluded him. Atlantis isn't lurking here in Southwark. I had suspected as much.

He runs a hand through his hair and fidgets with his measuring tape.

I didn't sufficiently defend its integrity. The outside no longer reveals what is going on inside. In the initial plans, the different functions of each part of the building were to be transparent. I wanted people on the outside to be able to see in. The transitions from offices to shops to apartments to the terrace were apparent, and now they're invisible. There had been plans to put in, among other things, an auditorium, but we never did. What bothers me is the sensation that, beyond the façade, there is not enough depth.

The Shard is a bit tame compared to its initial design.

I keep picturing it as wilder, maybe a touch more innocent.

That happens. Over time designs get diluted.

The Fox and the Tower

Let me tell you the story of Romeo the fox. While construction was underway, Romeo elected to build his den on the 72nd floor. Whether he had come to the city to escape royal hunting parties or was himself hunting for food, we never found out. He ate what the workers left him. By day he toddled up and down the stairs and at night slept on a pallet. The Shard and its 1,500 workers from sixty different countries adopted him. As a consequence, Romeo enjoyed a vast menu. He was fed everything from couscous to fish and chips.

After months of freeloading, he was captured by the animal protection services, which let him loose in the countryside, where a fox belongs. The veterinarian who opened the cage said that before trotting off into the woods, Romeo turned, pricked up his ears and gazed one last time at the tower.

My father likes to think that, now and again, the fox returns to admire his skyscraper, perhaps from the distant heath he now calls home.

The Shard can be seen from anywhere in London. According to pilots, when they fly into the city, the Shard is often the one building penetrating the clouds.
It's also a reliable landmark for those navigating the city on foot.

Our launch is pulling ashore. There are many ships on the river today, like in the paintings of Canaletto. Or the age of the Great Tea Race, when clippers used to race from Shanghai to London. Whoever arrived first fetched a higher price for their precious load of tea. The ships were used to transport other less cumbersome and highly profitable goods too, like spices, silk, and wool. They were extremely fast and, given their fine-lined hulls that clipped through the waves, had narrow cargo holds.

With the trade winds behind them, a clipper could cover fifteen thousand miles in a hundred days. Occasionally, after more than three months at sea, they would reach the port within a few hours of one another. Equipped with three masts, they were the most technically advanced naval ships before steamships came along and replaced them. They sailed the longest and most dangerous routes, from Sydney or Shanghai to London, from New York to San Francisco by way of Cape Horn.

Names like *Thermopylae* and *Cutty Sark* are inscribed in the annals of seafaring, as is *Torrens*, a ship that embarked from Plymouth and Port Adelaide and on which Joseph Conrad served as chief officer. A clipper could sail at fifteen knots and, in the right conditions, reach speeds of up to twenty knots, whereas other ships sailed at a mere five. They had a superior sail area but that made them difficult to maneuver. Veteran captains and experienced sailors were required to put a clipper out to sea.

The Sermon

A whole world spins underneath the Shard, teeming with black cabs, red double-deckers, packs of bicyclists and herds of pedestrians. Three hundred thousand passengers a day pass through London Bridge station. There are also two subway lines. Someone once wrote that the Shard is a monument to London's commuters.

Before we got started, Livingstone made one demand: no parking lots. He wanted visitors to use the public transit system that he was committed to improving.

His proviso made me smile. Today there are only parking spaces for disabled drivers and emergency vehicles. See that white stone church, to the right, on Montague Close? That is where I gave my sermon on the Shard.

The sermon is news to me. He points to Southwark's cathedral, not as grand an edifice as you might think. Actually, it is a small Gothic building. Its full name is the Cathedral and Collegiate Church of St. Saviour and St. Mary Overie, but no one has the patience to call it that. Here is where the Old Man spoke to its congregants.

Small maybe, but venerable. Given its history, and its popularity. The bishop, who supported the building of the Shard, invited me to explain to residents how the design would impact them and their neighborhood. I spoke about how the Shard could usher in a renaissance.

I remember the church was full. Young people crouched on the floor and listened, others sat on the entrance steps. At the time we faced hostility in London, on account of opposition from certain associations, English Heritage in particular. They objected that the building was too modern, that it would dwarf the dome of St. Paul's Cathedral, one of the city's symbols.

Others attacked me for the shape of the skyscraper, saying it was too pointed or too big or too transparent or disproportionately large. The truth is that the Shard is startlingly different, but so are the ships on the Thames. Even Westminster Abbey catches us off guard.

Cities are full of surprising presences. And it takes time for a surprising building to be embraced and loved.

Before construction could begin, they conducted a long public inquiry. In Great Britain trials of that nature precede all major public works. Finally, after various hearings, my father managed to break ground. When he went to Westminster to show his design to the parliamentary committee, he wore under his jacket a T-shirt that read, "Trust me, I am an architect."

Sure, several other people besides myself went to testify at the court on St. Thomas Street. I found myself in the middle of a real court case, with a prosecution, a defense, and witnesses.

We won the trial by arguing that, in the middle of the 1600s, despite obstruction from traditionalists, Christopher Wren had managed to carry out his own modern project, St. Paul's.

On November 21, 2003, the sentence came down approving the Shard. "My decision may be biased," added the judge, "because I like the project."

Emperor Claudius' Villa

During excavations they discovered something that had been

buried underground for two thousand years, dating back to the time Claudius conquered Britain and founded Londinium. What they turned up were the ruins of a Roman villa replete with crockery and an entire arsenal of household appurtenances, material proof that the city's history began here in Southwark.

Digging turns up all sorts of things. That is what I mean when I say architecture is an adventurous profession.

You're in London putting up a skyscraper and suddenly you stumble upon a Roman villa, as I did in Rome while excavating the foundation of the Auditorium. But in the Eternal City you expect to find a villa from the fifth century B.C.

In Athens, we came across a cemetery for prisoners.

In Berlin, Russian bombs that had failed to detonate. We anticipated finding oil fields in the center of Los Angeles, not mammoth skeletons.

In Beirut, we turned up Phoenician walls and capitals.

In Amiens discovered underground bat caves where human beings had most likely never set foot.

You find everything when you're excavating to lay the foundations. Hence my belief that sooner or later we'll find Atlantis.

Building the Shard was an adventure for other reasons. At the top of the building, where wind speeds exceed eighty kilometers per hour, the crew was composed of professional climbers. They would walk around the construction site in mountain-climbing gear, harnesses and carabiners hanging off them. While everyone else rode the elevator, they would climb seventy flights as a warm-up.

Above, twenty mountaineers were climbing around; below, construction miners cleared debris from the river.

Do you know why the construction miners and mountain climbers were working in tandem?

In an urban environment you can't have trucks hauling around dirt all day, polluting the air. You have to invent certain systems.

At the Shard we used the top-down method, which essentially amounts to having climbers build above ground while miners lay the foundations. Trees grow the same way: as the trunk gets taller, the roots burrow into the ground.

For urban rock climbers, tightrope walkers, and protestors, skyscrapers are like honey. A few years after the inauguration, six Greenpeace activists tried to scale the Shard to protest oil drilling. But they stopped halfway up, exhausted from the exertion. They got stuck at the fortieth floor. The same mountain climbers who built the Shard had to come in and escort them to the top, where the activists were finally able to unfurl their flag.

One man who was stopped before he had the chance was the famous *grimpeur* Alain Robert, a kind of spider man who had previously climbed the *New York Times* tower. The police identified him in the hall of the Shard and, by special ordinance, forbid him from approaching the building.

Alain often and reluctantly lands in prison. As happened in Manhattan, where anti-terrorist teams were waiting for him on the roof, and at the Aurora Place in Sydney. For reasons unbeknownst to me, he is obsessed with the Constructor's buildings. Apparently, under the guise of a journalist, he once gained access to the atelier in Paris to steal details pertaining to handholds in the facades. He plans his schemes scrupulously. He is, in his way, a scientist.

Alain made it clear that if my father intended to design a building that was impossible to climb, he had to talk to Alain. Alain would tell him how.

Arianna's Paper

It is six in the evening and pedestrians are funneling into the jaws of London Bridge station. The time has come for us to get back on board too. As we wait for our launch, my father extracts yet another slip of paper from his pocket. The paper is by Arianna, a student. I am not sure whether she is in her first year of high school or her last of middle school.

This summer I went to my favorite city, London. The day before leaving, my family and I rode to the top of the Shard, the tallest skyscraper in Europe. The building shot up out of the ground where you'd least expect. The London sky was, as usual, gray, but above the building was a gash of blue shaped like a star. The enormous glass shard was so tall it looked as if it could touch the sky and part the clouds. The skyscraper dominates the city. Hard to miss a thousand-foot crystal! We took the elevator and climbed to the top. I was really excited. As soon as I reached the top floor, I noticed those amazing windows. I walked toward them and looked out over London. I saw lots of tiny people and thought to myself, each of them has a life full of uncertainties, fears, pains, joys, and happiness. I realized the world works like an ant farm: every ant does their little job, but that job can help make a better world. I realized even the smallest person can do great things in life. Of course, you need to work hard, but that is an obstacle that you can overcome, and anyway it's indispensable to pushing ahead. So I stood at the window for fifteen minutes thinking these thoughts and then, with a heavy heart, took the elevator down to the ground floor to catch the Tube.[11]

---

[11] The authors thank Arianna for her beautiful paper. To protect her privacy, her last name has been omitted.

13.
SWAMP THING

We cross the Channel on an early March night, under a starry sky. Ideal conditions for sailing by the stars, for putting yourself in the hands of the celestial bodies. Their position in relation to Earth is calculated for specific dates and times and published in the nautical almanac, a kind of Bible for sailors that tabulates the hourly angles of the sun and moon, and the ascent of the sixty-six most important stars. The boatswain claims that the Milky Way, Cassiopeia, and Ursa Major are the most reliable guides, better than satellite systems, which can always break down.

The moon illuminates the sea gently, unlike the harsh light of the sun. Orbiting behind the moon, hidden in a bend in space, was asteroid number 216241, christened Renzopiano. The Explorer hadn't discovered it; he hasn't ventured out into the cosmos just yet. The International Astronomical Union of Boston notified him.

The asteroid was discovered by Silvano Casulli, an Italian astronomer, on November 14, 2006, at the Vallemare di Borbona observatory. Castulli is the one who named it. I don't know why he chose the name, but I am grateful to him.

The asteroid is located in the main asteroid belt, between Mars and Jupiter. Its orbital period, the time it takes to make a complete orbit, is about two years, and it has a diameter of four to five kilometers. The International Astronomical Union has been keeping an eye on the Renzopiano asteroid for a while, to ensure it doesn't present a danger to our planet.

They have observed it 125 times since 2006. Enough times to confirm that it would not collide with Earth for at least two million years. It feels strange to be connected to that gigantic rock rolling around in outer space.

To reach Paris we have to travel up the Seine, but at three meters and sixty centimeters, the keel of the *Magnaghi* sits too deep for us to pass without snagging on the riverbed. The mouth of the river is on the other side of the Channel, near Le Havre, a route that we can sail as far as Rouen. From there we will have to be transported by a barge that can wend its way upriver.

What brings us to Paris? The Pompidou mostly, where our search probably should have begun. The Constructor had pursued Atlantis a long time ago, in the Marais, where he landed that strange, bright, tubular spaceship.

There is something else I want to see. The Institut du Monde Arabe is opening an exhibit on Heracleion and Canopus, two Egyptian cities that were once submerged in the Nile Delta. Archaeologists had recovered all sorts of relics, coins, the stele of Pharaoh Nectanebo I, sacred objects, and a statue of the god Hapi, the personification of annual flooding.

Forty Years On

The Pompidou opened on January 31, 1977, over forty years ago. I was still a boy, but I was there. Clenching a pipe and wrapped in a herringbone coat, my father carried Lia on his shoulders, because she was small and risked being trampled by the crowd. Back then the Old Man, hardly old at the time, had a long black beard.

I remember traveling up the clear escalator: flight after flight you discovered a new piece of Paris.

A lot of people came to gaze at that bizarre urban machine— exactly how many we never found out. At a certain point they were forced to block the entrance owing to the size of the crowd. The morning after, fifteen people were found inside; they had gotten lost and spent the night in makeshift beds, some on the terrace and some in the atrium. Since then, the building has received over twenty thousand visitors a day.

Valéry Giscard d'Estaing performed the ceremony, because Georges Pompidou, who had campaigned to build the center, had died three years earlier. Hence the building is called the Centre Pompidou, though for us it will always be Beaubourg.

I hadn't yet turned twelve, so my memory of that time is hazy. Here an image, there a black hole. That explains why, before embarking on this periplus, knowing that I would have time to read, I asked my mother for her recollections. She had written me a letter, which I have yet to open, but now, rocked by the waves of the Channel, I will.

Dear Carlo,

I used to tell you fairytales to get you to sleep, to little avail. Now I figure I will tell you about a few times that you and I spent together. The story begins when you were four years old. I hope it won't put you to sleep. It is the story of our adventure in London and Paris, and the fairytale that was the Centre Pompidou. You told me you might stop there on your trip with your father.

I'll tell you about London, because that is where the project began. Why am I telling you about Beaubourg? Because it marked a real turn in your father's career and a radical change in our lives. In 1968 your father already had contacts in London. Beginning in the 1960s, the city had seen an explosion of innovations in music, art, architecture, film, and fashion, and was a breeding ground for his brand of architecture. Besides, working in Italy was a challenge.

Genoa was stuck, and the country slow. One day your father asked me, in his terse way, "What if we left?" I didn't even ask where to. "Yes, let's get out of here!" I told him. So, we loaded a few things into the old ramshackle Fiat 1100. One of the side doors kept opening on its own. Ah, I almost forgot, we also packed you and Matteo into the car. He would have been a little over a year.

What I remember about London, besides my discovery of miniskirts, is an exhibit of your father's in Olympia Hall, in 1966, called "Architectural Research by Renzo Piano." To prepare for the journey, we had taken English lessons in Genoa, which turned out to be pretty useless. I am telling you about this because for me that conference your father held in 1966 was unforgettable. He appeared on stage, surrounded by his designs and slides, and was applauded by the audience. But as soon as he started talking, the room became perplexed by his fanciful English. I noticed a few ironic British smirks, but they quickly gave way to an interest in what he was saying, showing, miming, and shouting with incredible conviction. When it was over, he received a long round of applause, and I felt very proud.

Let's continue our journey, Carlo, shall we? Your dad had the same pluck as the Italian emigrants of the 1930s, as did I. When we arrived, I found London to be very beautiful. Our arrival was well planned, thanks, I believe, to Richard Rogers, with whom your father had already collaborated. Richard's mother and father were Italian.

In Richard I found the brother I never had, since I was an only daughter. Awaiting us was an apartment on a hill, which Richard had had repainted in a day by a warm group of students from Battersea College. The house was in Netherhall Gardens, in Hampstead, a neighborhood in the northwest of the city, at the top of a hill, up which, for the entire length of our stay, I would push a pram packed with groceries and the two of you. At the end of the street was a park, and I remember one cold day taking a family stroll with Richard, who had bought you both Scotch eggs, boiled and fried whole. Awful. At the time I got to know him, Richard was going through a rough patch with his wife Sue. I often walked in on her crying. She never confided in me what the problem was, but it wasn't hard to guess, and for me silence was easier to understand than an explanation in English.

They had three very beautiful boys who used to eat cucumbers with the wrapper on. I think they preferred the plastic. Sue was an intelligent woman with whom I became friends. She was a good cook and thanks to her I learned the proper way to prepare roast beef. But Sue was soon out of the picture. Enter Ruth, his second wife, completely different: American, exuberant, disorganized, friendly. It was clear that Richard and Ruth loved each other and were physically attracted to one another. I was even a little envious of this beautiful couple.

I remember the first dinner that Ruth prepared for us: the pièce de résistance was a Hamburg hen cooked with its entrails and wrapped in foil to keep from "losing its scent." Fortunately, I was seated next to an odd English architect, to whom I am eternally grateful. Seeing how slowly I was eating, he polished off my serving. Your father was busy talking about architecture and probably didn't even notice the smell and the taste. You know how his passion eclipses everything. Later, much to my surprise, Ruth became one of the best chefs in London, authored several cookbooks and managed a very popular restaurant on the Thames.

1968 Was the Year

Your dad had begun working with Richard, who soon proposed they become partners. Unlike your father, Richard was not a workaholic, but he was a sensible and kind person with a knack for sniffing out talent and finding excellent collaborators. So, between the end of 1968 and the start of 1969, Piano & Rogers was founded. That was when they decided to enter the competition to build the Centre Pompidou.

I used to hang out at the studio, which was a pleasant space to work on my dissertation on Viking sagas. And there I watched the project grow. They were rebellious times: 68 hung in the air, people were rejecting the pieties of mainstream culture, rejecting culture as a middle-class commodity to be displayed and sold at the supermarket. That was the first idea behind the design, though fortunately a few changes were made during the design phase. In the London studio the work was buoyed by all the boxes of wine given as gifts to Richard, who had already made a name for himself. The wine encouraged the positive atmosphere, the freedom to invent. And where were you and Matteo?

In the morning your father would take you to the English preschool, which periodically called us in on account of your extremely Italian behavior.

Apparently, you were aggressive with your native-born classmates, and Matteo would spend the day under the table, where it was impossible to get him out. But Matteo was happiest when we left you with the babysitter, an attractive, good-natured, plump blonde. He loved riding on her back and hugging her. He was already on the brink of becoming a *tombeur de femmes* in Paris. And then . . . I remember the three of us collecting stones and leaves, Sundays in the parks, especially the park with deer—Richmond Park I think it was called—the one your father liked best.

I still have a photo of a terrified, wide-eyed Matteo, with a large set of deer antlers behind him. Then there were our slow strolls along the Thames, observing the birds and fish, and having to keep you on a short leash because you wanted to catch them all. You may not remember, but one time I took you to Portobello Market, where I bought a large mirror for the house. But you had your eye on a large sword, which I had to purchase in order to get you to keep walking.

We got on the subway with mirror and sword, and at our stop, an English gentleman offered to carry the mirror for me. Like that, we made our way to the studio. When I thanked him and said goodbye, the gentleman was a bit crestfallen. We entered the studio, you brandishing your sword. Everybody but your father laughed. For your own safety, he quickly disposed of it.

I remember in July we decided to take a break; we all needed it. You and Matteo were to go to the countryside with your grandparents to recover from your clashes with the English children, reunite with your friends, regain your Mediterranean complexion and clear up the acne caused by all the fish and chips your dad fed you. Your parents were to take a well-deserved ten-day vacation in Greece, offered to me by your father. In the meantime, the design had been entered into the competition. We knew that it was a highly qualified international jury and that the French president would not, as was only right, be participating. Had he participated I don't think the Piano & Rogers Studio would have won. The jury was chaired by Jean Prouvé, a constructor, engineer, and architect, who was very interested in your father's works and experiments. In my opinion, there were so many lobbyists in that competition that they may have cancelled one another out. The studio had no references.

I was happy, but on the morning of July 16, 1971, while I was packing our bags in Genoa, the telephone rang, and I answered. The call was from Paris. A woman's voice told me, "Renzo Piano *est le lauréat*." Stunned, I replied that of course he had graduated—from the Polytechnic University of Milan *avec incroyable* grades, and, if they wanted, I could mail them a copy of his diploma. After a puzzled silence, she repeated, "*Pas lauréat, lauréat!*" A doubt crept in. I called your father, who came downstairs in his underwear, took hold of the receiver, and, after talking for a moment, sat there on the floor, in silence, still clutching the receiver. He had just been told that their design for Beaubourg had won. Shock. Joy. A phone call to Richard.

I have to confess I felt a petty little pang of regret for Greece, which was fading into the distance.

Yet, perhaps because nothing was imminent, or because he felt sorry for me, or perhaps because, ever the thrifty Genoese, he knew the tickets and reservations were not refundable, your father said, "We're going anyway." I am still grateful to him for that gift. Naturally, we had to cut short our vacation: two days in Athens with a trip to the Parthenon at two in the afternoon in thirty-eight-degree weather. My idea. Followed by an excursion to Aegina, where I had to jump into the sea after being chased by a goat while trying to pick figs on the beach. Your father was silent. It made sense, since, at thirty-three, he was about to embark on an incredible adventure. His silence led me to understand our vacation was nearing its end. He bought me a white sheepskin coat that I wore for the entire time I was in Paris. It smelled of Greece, vacation, and goats.

Victorious, me happy because I had almost finished my dissertation, you and your brother a little worn-out but having survived, we returned to London, this time by plane. It was your first flight. You were your usual lively self, and Matteo was calm, but when he asked me where the legs of the plane were, and we laughed and told him there weren't any, he panicked. From London we returned to Genoa. I took you two to the countryside in San Luca, and your dad and Richard dashed off to Paris. That was the start of their adventure . . .

The letter continues, but the boatswain has just now swept into the bunk. He had been relieved of his watch and, given the fury with which he slammed the door behind him, isn't in the best of moods. With not so much as a good night, unless you can call a grunt a good night, he switches off the blue light of his table lamp and buries himself under the covers. I'll keep reading at a more opportune time.

Armilla

When Beaubourg was nearly finished, the director Roberto Rossellini came to shoot a documentary. His crew installed microphones in all of the rooms, where the eye of the camera roamed silently. Rather than actors, Rossellini cast unsuspecting visitors, ordinary people who found themselves for the first time coming into contact with contemporary art. The master of neorealism was giving voice to the public's astonishment. He filmed what he saw, recorded what he heard. It was his last work, since he died suddenly a few months later, in June 1977. I believe it was his son who completed shooting and edited *Beaubourg*.

During filming, Rossellini gave my father a piece of invaluable advice: "If you want to know if you've done a good job, Renzo, don't look at the building. Look at the eyes of the people looking at it."

My father took that lesson to heart: after he completes a project, he never fails to hide behind a column and observe the looks on people's faces. He has learned how to catch the building's reflection in their gazes.

On the construction site, characters came and went. Even

Mr. Honda showed up on a visit from Japan. "I like it," he said. "It looks like one of my motorcycles."

Italo Calvino, who at the time was living in Paris, was one of the most frequent visitors. Calvino was always carrying a notebook with him, which he filled with tiny, cramped notes. He may be the reason the Constructor became fixated with carrying around a sheet of paper every day to scribble down notes and sketches. Every evening he rereads that day's page, files it away someplace, and dogears another for the next.

He and Calvino hung out. I know the writer used to make crazy proposals. For instance, he suggested they clean the facades of Beaubourg with giant automated brushes, the kind you find at a carwash, only much bigger.

One of Calvino's "invisible cities"—the book was published by Einaudi around that time—is called Armilla, and it sounds a lot like Beaubourg. It is a construction site where only plumbers work. They keep waiting for bricklayers who never show. In the end, Armilla is colonized by naiads, nymphs of running water.

I think he already had the idea, he may have even written it. But there is something of Beaubourg in that story and there is something of Armilla in the building we designed.

He pulls out a photocopy of Calvino's page from his binder. He reads it aloud. At the top of his lungs, actually. He has to, otherwise nature will drown him out. The wind scatters his words to the surf as the Channel begins to foam.

Whether Armilla is like this because it is unfinished or because it has been demolished, whether the cause is some enchantment or only a whim, I do not know. The fact remains that it has no walls, no ceilings, no floors: it has nothing that makes it seem a city, except the water pipes that rise vertically where the houses should be and spread out horizontally where the floors should be: a forest of pipes that end in taps, showers, spouts, overflows . . .[12]

Je Ne Comprends Pas

Whether Beaubourg came first or Armilla, I don't know. Actually, they may have been born at the same time. Something was changing: those were the years of protests, the counterculture movement, Woodstock, free love, and student revolutions.

The notes of the Beatles' psychedelic *Yellow Submarine* resound in the large pipes of Calvino's imaginary city and the large pipes of the Constructor's *bâtiment*.

As my mother said, he had taken us all to London, where my father taught in a school of architecture for a time. He would assemble and dismantle structures with his students in the public gardens. All in the span of half a day. End of lesson, go in peace.

Lia hadn't been born yet. I hardly remember a thing, except going to preschool and getting into fights with my English friends. But let's get one thing straight: they were always the ones who started it. I remember my father prohibiting me from getting close to his models, because whatever I touched, I wound up smashing. But this tale of the little destroyer never totally convinced me.

I still have an image of my parents dressed in bellbottoms and flashy knit sweaters. Richard was the same way; they were hippies and rebels. Beaubourg is a 1968 project, created elsewhere.

The idea of erecting a building complex, however cultural

---

[12] Italo Calvino, *Invisible Cities*, translated by William Weaver (Harcourt Inc., 1978)

it may be, in the posh center of the Ville Lumière, was seen as a challenge, almost an offense. Back then museums were dreary, dusty, decidedly unattractive places. My father and Richard were young and maybe a bit irreverent. But you have to admit, there was one thing they had understood: it made no sense to build another temple. In fact, Beaubourg was considered an affront. Perhaps an affront is what was called for; there was no shortage of godliness.

Every time I walk by, I still can't believe they were allowed to make it. He and Richard didn't have the faintest hope of winning the competition. Six hundred eighty-one architectural firms had participated, they were not much older than thirty, and after delivering their design they went back to their small jobs without giving it another thought. They were practically unemployed, as architects.

Up until that moment I had performed experiments. I had been playing with structures, with materials and shapes.

Those were important years spent trying and trying over, even if I wasn't constructing buildings intended to last. I was producing pieces. I wasn't an architect in the classic sense of the word. With Beaubourg I was hoping to put all the pieces together. That's it. I was hoping that my passion would turn into a building.

Experimenting helped me in many respects. Knowing how to make things not only with your mind but with your hands is liberating. If you try to use a material, an element, or a technique in a way that it isn't meant to be used, there always comes a time when you are told it can't be done.

While we were building Beaubourg, we had to realize a structure in cast steel, but we ran into a problem with the French construction industry, which was hostile.

In the end the order was placed with the Krupp company, in Germany. I can't tell you the controversy that caused.

These steel beams, fifty meters long and weighing 120 tons, arrived in the middle of the night. They were practically smuggled in and assembled immediately.

According to Jean Prouvé, the chair of the jury, when they opened the sealed envelope and read the name Piano & Rogers, an embarrassing silence fell over the room. No one had the faintest idea who they were.

Harboring no expectations, they took a stab, unafraid of having made a mistake. The risk paid off.

I still don't understand why they let us do it. We were two stubborn kids smashing walls. We doubled down on our disobedience, using our ignorance of French as an excuse so that they would leave us in peace.

Je ne comprends pas—that was our motto. Sorry, I don't understand, and therefore I will go on doing things my way.

Before then I had never worked on a project that lasted for more than six months. President Pompidou was well aware of that fact. At our first meeting he told us, "You do understand, sirs, that this building has to last five hundred years?"

And so it shall. Though by all appearances Beaubourg remains a temporary structure.

Sins of Youth

After the Paris adventure he spent years defending himself against people who feared they would put pipes up everywhere. Rogers suffered the same fate, a fate reserved for heretics during the Middle Ages. Well, maybe heretics had it worse.

On one wet and windy occasion, a woman was crossing the Place Pompidou when her umbrella turned inside out, and

Richard kindly helped her re-right it. The woman thanked him, but when she learned that he and his friend were the architects of the *raffinerie*, she clamped shut her umbrella and began shaking it at their heads.

They called it all sorts of names: a refinery, a factory, a car tower, a cultural supermarket, a disgrace. Most of the names were mean, and that left us a little bitter, but the feeling passed.

Or maybe it didn't pass, but we were too busy to let it faze us. We wanted to make a factory that responded to the needs and changes in culture.

We were attracted to the iconoclastic idea of a factory. We carried on, stubborn as teenagers.

I remember how, at the conference to present the project, the public shouted at us to go home, that we ought to be ashamed. We were at the Grand Palais. I had to do the talking, because I was the one who spoke a little French. I had carefully prepared what I wanted to say: it was important. I explained to the indignant crowd that we wanted Beaubourg to be a cross between the Louvre and Times Square. I kept thanking them: *merci, merci, merci.* But they took a completely different view of things.

We were reckless, the two of us.

The building was given the most outrageous nicknames. The Plant, the Gasometer, Notre Dame of the Pipes, the Monster of the Marais, i.e., swamp thing (*marais* means swamp in French). Residents collected thirty thousand signatures in protest and had an eloquent flier printed up. "It may be a refined masterpiece of rational expression," it read, "but we don't give a crap."

A rumor was going around the city that Les Halles, the historic market in Paris, was going to be demolished to make room for Beaubourg. The truth is that all that had stood on the site was a parking lot, while Les Halles was on the other side of the boulevard de Sébastopol, what is now the Forum shopping center.

There was a sea change in Parisians' attitude toward Beaubourg. At first there was a clear divide between those who admired it and those who detested it. But far more people were in the second camp.

Over time those numbers were flipped. After all, every new building has the serious disadvantage of being new, of having yet to fall into step with the city. It takes time to acclimate.

When architecture heralds the future and embodies change, it inevitably becomes the target of criticism.

But architecture is not new for the sake of provoking people. It is new because the world it represents has changed. I listen to dissenting opinions; I have always listened to them, I welcome them if they help me improve.

We started with the idea of opening up to the city, and Beaubourg established certain things that can be found in all of my subsequent museums: accessibility and transparency. Light and transparency, which I may have drawn from the sea, with its special radiance and colors. I like to think of my museums as ships at a standstill.

And yet even in Paris, on the Plateau Beaubourg, I am sure some detail doesn't sit right with him. An idea unfinished, a dream unrealized and lost in the process . . .

I have no major regrets, though for a long time I had my doubts. That's true. Richard was always more confident than me, more certain.

What fails to convince me is the later addition in the square, which looks like the work of someone who wanted to atone for a sin he'd committed in his youth. I mean the IRCAM (Institut de Recherche et Coordination Acoustique/Musique) tower, where the offices and the Atelier Brancusi are located. They're almost afterthoughts, the work of someone who has been browbeaten and is trying to set things right.

Brancusi disappears. IRCAM is made of terracotta. It almost ingratiates itself with the older buildings surrounding it, and it isn't, as it ought to be, in conversation with Beaubourg.

Both lack courage. Were I to build them today, I would design them as fragments of Beaubourg scattered around the square.

Every time he passes by he says he's returning to the scene of the crime. Almost as if it were the work of youthful excess. Some critics have criticized him by saying his work post Pompidou is a form of reparation, that he has corrected the past by throwing himself into endeavors that are poles apart: taking on the role of archidoctor, erecting unobtrusive construction sites, opening the workshop, carrying out urban renewal projects, salvaging buildings.

It wasn't atonement. I was launching into direct contact with people. That was the idea behind the open construction site in Otranto. An architect who listens and engages people before stepping in. The use of diagnostics to be as effective as possible and not trample residents. Not tear them from their homes during construction. Science at the service of the community.

In a sense I was returning to my roots, to my first experiments. Getting back to people and the construction site again, the small construction site. After an experience as overwhelming as Beaubourg, I needed to. My first real project did not come until the Menil Collection in Houston, a museum neither big nor commemorative.

When Dominique de Menil came to Paris in the fall of 1980, she invited me to her home in rue Saint-Dominique. "I don't like Beaubourg," she told me, "but I like how you approached the idea of a new cultural center. I admire the free spirit with which you embarked on this adventure. You acted in a fresh and liberating manner, which is why I am confident that you'll do the same with my project. I want a building that's big on the inside but discreet on the outside."

Mascaret

Embarking on the first leg of the Seine, you need to keep an eye out for the *mascaret*, or tidal bore. The word *mascaret* was new to me, because, in part, the Mediterranean has been spared the phenomenon. A *mascaret* is a wave that travels upriver. At high tide, when the sea level rises at the mouth of a river, a kind of backflow spreads upstream. It was hazardous until the 1960s, when a system of dams was built to restrict the flow of water.

There is a tragic story involving *mascarets*. On September 4, 1843, at Villequier, the wave sank a boat carrying Léopoldine Hugo, the daughter of Victor Hugo, and her husband Charles Vacquerie. The couple drowned.

But all you need to do is calculate the tides. No one on deck is troubled. The Old Man least of all. He resumes his story.

Richard and I were a perfect match to work on Beaubourg.

Two young guys passionate about building, impelled by society, high on hope. On utopia too, perhaps.

At first Richard was the one who poured his soul into the project, and his passion became mine. The idea of a flexible building that could be transformed over time described our own faith in a culture capable of reinventing itself.

Culture as an accomplishment that a community either is or is not capable of. When it is, the spaces dedicated to it must be ready to welcome it and follow it whither it wanders, must be able to transform themselves.

That explains why we rotated everything that is normally fixed in place—the infrastructure, the elevators, the escalators, the piping—and put it outside the building. To leave the central area free and flexible.

In *Foucault's Pendulum* Umberto Eco reimagines the great air ducts appearing in the square as portholes through which the underworld communicates with the land of the living. On more than one occasion I heard the Surveyor call them ears. For me they resemble nautical windsocks, taking air into the lungs of the building.

Sitting on an incline, like a Greek amphitheater, this square has faint echoes of many places, including the Piazza del Campo in Siena.

There was also the iconoclastic wish to breathe new life into the basements with our giant airducts. When the workers started assembling them, the city's prefect became furious. He intervened, saying that we had gone too far, that a line had been crossed. We were forced to bring them back to the warehouse, but after three months we tried to install them again.

This time the prefect became even more livid. He sent a messenger to tell us we had gone too far and that he had about run out of patience. He swore he would never allow it. "*Jamais, moi vivant!*"

Once again we had to retrace our steps. Things went on like that for a year. Until one day we received the sad news that he had died.

The next day we installed the airducts, and they are still there. It took our recklessness plus the courage of the French government to pull it off. Pompidou had appointed Jean Prouvé to be president of the competition, and Prouvé was further removed from the academy than any man I've ever known.

There were many other freethinkers, like Robert Bordaz, who presided over the design, and Pontus Hultén, who directed the museum.

There was Jean Tinguely, who used scraps from the building to make sculptures, and occasionally carried off good pieces too. It was a pioneering age, and we were a wild bunch. In order for us to practice in France President Pompidou had to issue an administrative order declaring that we were, indeed, architects, and could legally practice there.

Six lawsuits attempted to block construction, some on trumped-up charges. Academics argued that placing a structure with exposed tubes a step away from the Gothic church of Saint-Merri was sacrilege.

But Bordaz had an inspired idea: he claimed the design was actually Gothic in vision and that the standing tubes mirrored the spires of Saint-Merri.

A colossal lie. Bordaz was a genius.

A newspaper published an open letter by intellectuals railing against Beaubourg. It wasn't a fake. The text was by Parisian intellectuals against the Eiffel Tower. They had faithfully copied out the entire letter from the nineteenth century, except they had changed the names of the signatories and replaced the Eiffel Tower with Beaubourg. One powerful group hostile to the project had the nerve to call themselves Le Comité pour le Geste Architectural.

Our trip up the river is proceeding without a hitch, the waters slow and smooth, nothing like our rollercoaster ride across the Atlantic. The Seine zigzags, like a snake looking for a route to the North Sea. We are traveling against the current toward Paris.

The barge we boarded in Rouen glides gently along too, grinding out the miles to Île-de-France. Its name is Atalanta, like the nymph daughter of the king of Arcadia.

We see the steep banks of Les Andelys topped by the ruins of Richard the Lionhearted's castle. We see the Oise sidle into the Seine in Conflans-Sainte-Honorine, dotted with blooming apple trees. We hear black geese honking in Duclair.

Acrobats

Now that we are in Paris, I almost regret having to leave the peaceful Atalanta in the harbor of Gennevilliers. But the Seine has not abandoned us; it turns up at every corner.

In the square of Beaubourg an Andean is playing the transverse flute, acrobats are twirling in a semicircle of onlookers, and a girl is blowing a titanic soap bubble. It is almost as if the square reconciles two worlds: the physical world of the building and neighborhood, and the symbolic world of culture and street life. Mimes, fire eaters, dancers, and traveling musicians take turns on their cobblestone stage.

A few months ago I saw a César exhibit at the Beaubourg. A lot of people came to look at his sculptures, in part because it was the museum's free day.

Crushed cars, expansions of polyurethane foam. César made sculptures out of scraps and trash he salvaged from landfills. He used to say that he was poor and Carrara marble too expensive. The crowd that day was made up not of experts but of people searching for the ghost that each sculpture conjures.

People visit museums to dream, to interrogate themselves, to observe. They are places where miracles happen.

For a young person, a drawing, a flattened car, a sketch, a sentence, or a series of musical notes can mark the start of their creative life. That occurs if the museum succeeds in making people feel something.

I see Beaubourg as a joyful urban machine, which inspires more than a few questions.

After it opened there was talk of fencing off the square, for security reasons. I used to listen to my father protest, because doing so would have meant separating the building from the city. They were afraid of assemblies and riots. The gendarmerie believed it dangerous to open the square to everyone. But ultimately they didn't build the fence.

Still, the building seems to have been, over time, betrayed. The wide-open spaces broken up into rooms, the moving walls made more static. People were barred from riding the escalator without a ticket; to enjoy the view at the top you had to pay. Only now, perhaps, will it return to being free.

The metal detectors installed after the terrorist attacks in France also act as a barrier between the outside and inside. In short, the myth of a building that is open to the city, that is part of the city, what the two men had imagined, is at risk of being repressed.

We stopped the square from being cordoned off. But I was wrong to have let the units in the lobby fill up; they were protected urban spaces. I regret it, because they had been conceived of as open to and in dialogue with the city. Then they disappeared to make more room for the museum.

I shouldn't have allowed them to be closed. In part, the building broke its promise to be open to everyone. The unfortunate fate of buildings born wild is that they become tamed.

I'm afraid I have not fought hard enough.

Baptiste's Beaubourg

When I was a kid, on Sundays my parents would take me to Crêperie Bretonne, a small restaurant in the square, on the corner of rue Saint-Merri. We lived nearby. We would stroll around while my father had a look at the construction site. I liked ham and cheese crepes, but my mother always ordered spinach. After all, vegetables are good for you.

They also served cider on tap. Two types, actually. Sweet and dry. I preferred dry cider, and my parents let me drink it because it have a low alcohol content. The crêperie is now gone, so we have to make do with a normal bistro. My father passes me a letter mailed to his studio in the rue des Archives by a man named Baptiste.[13]

Good day Sir,

I am delighted to write you. I have worked at the Centre Pompidou for twenty-five years, and for twenty-five years I have been happy working here. In my role as director of the DDC/Les Cinémas, I toggle between working in my office and taking frequent trips around the building.

Rather than relate the success of our cultural programming, I want to tell you about my personal relationship with the building.

It is always with a light heart that I set foot in the Centre. I like strolling through the halls, the walkways, entering the offices, riding the service elevators (and getting stuck), wandering through the library, bumping into friends at the coffee machines, not only on the top floors but also in the basement and parking lot. I like hearing the snore of the air conditioning. I like finding myself in the building late at night, all alone, after the public has gone, after all the night-shifts my work requires but never demands.

In this building I have dined on oysters for Christmas, in the theater below the Garange Room; I have slept, drank

[13] The authors thank Baptiste for his letter. To protect his privacy, his last name has been omitted.

(often), voted in the general assemblies, gone on strike, ridden a bicycle (it's true!), dressed up for the fashion show for the China exhibit to celebrate the building's thirtieth anniversary, collected the red ashtrays from the containers in the parking lot, courted women, and more . . . I have lived here, I live here, and I will live here for the entirety of my working life.

As the Centre approaches forty, I wanted to thank you and Richard Rogers, from the bottom of my heart, for this building, which has been a big part of my life, as it has been for millions of other people.

The evening lights make Beaubourg look like the factory it has always aspired to be. On the plateau, the artist Xavier Vielhan has erected steel statues of my father and Rogers, one light green, the other dark. They are set on two pedestals, Richard standing with his hands in his pockets and my father perched on a stool. The two statues make me laugh. The Explorer smiles, too. I know they embarrass him a little. So he changes the subject.

Nothing in the world is as powerful as an idea whose time has come. I'm not sure how true that is of the idea for Beaubourg, but the center is the one physical testimony to 1968 left in Paris.

I always wondered what my father thought of Beaubourg and what I was up to.

My relationship with him did not involve a lot of talking. He, too, was thrifty with his words. So, I would look to my mother to figure out what he thought. For her, it was a stroke of genius, but my father was never so forthcoming. Deep down I don't believe he disliked it. It is the work of a builder, same as him on his construction sites. I'd like to think he was quietly proud.

The next stop on our trip is Berlin, sea or no sea. To catch a glimpse of the Baltic you have to travel almost two hundred miles. But Paris has no sea either, nor is it hiding Atlantis. At least as Plato describes it. We will leave by train from Gare de l'Est for an eight-hour trip, changing trains in Düsseldorf, on the banks of the Rhine.

14

THE RETURN OF THE BLUE ANGEL

G hosts haunt the sky over Berlin. In this city, someone once said, nothing is more conspicuous than that which people seek to erase.

Thirty years ago, Potsdamer Platz was an empty region swarming with spirits too. We stop in front of the Weinhaus Huth, the one building left standing after the apocalyptic bombings of 1945. The attic windows of the pale stone building appear to pry into the life of the square, the beating heart of the capital, where once *Damen* in jewels met *Herren* in waistcoats, fashionable stores were opened, cars circulated, and people abandoned themselves to music and more or less lawful games.

It was here that the first public lighting system in Europe illuminated the night, here at this intersection that the prototype of the traffic light made its debut. Red, orange, and green stood side by side in a row. Berliners called it the *Oberkieker*, the lookout post. The year was 1924. Five heavily trafficked, arterial roads poured through Potsdamer Platz.

The Weinhaus Huth was a restaurant, the hangout of high-ranking party officials during the Nazi regime. Goebbels was a regular in the 1930s, and Alois Hitler, a man whose last name would later prove a burden, waited tables. Alois was the half-brother of the Führer, and given the outcome of the war, he wisely decided to change his name to Hiller. In a strange twist of history, he was put on trial. For, of all things, bigamy.

Do you know why the Weinhaus was spared? It's an odd story that I heard through the grapevine, but I think it's true: apparently the Weinhaus stored wine and beer on the roof, along with water, so when the bombs began to fall, the barrels burst and doused the fire.

The Weinhaus Huth was the headquarters of our first office for the Potsdamer Platz project. During construction it was set on stilts, so that we could keep working on the building engineering systems and the streets below. We had just six years to rebuild a piece of the city. There was practically nothing left but a no-man's-land separating East Berlin from West Berlin. But this building isn't the only surviving testament to the tragic conflict and delirium of the Cold War.

He points to two rows of linden trees, laden with yellow foliage, on the Alte Potsdamer Straße. To protect them during construction, the trees were wrapped in metal sheeting. Nothing but the branches remained exposed. They looked like they were wearing suits of armor.

In their shade, George Grosz had sketched his caricatures, the bitter scenes of the postwar period: streets, hovels, and living rooms vivisected by his pitiless pencil. Grosz met an unheroic end: drunk, staggering home in the middle of the night, he mistook the cellar door for the entrance.

Not far from Potsdamer Platz is the Führerbunker, where Hitler and Eva Braun lived out their last days. A plaque was not placed until 2006, either because the location of the bunker was unknown or because it was kept a secret to avoid its becoming a pilgrimage site for fanatics.

Trabants

We have a look around. The place seems to pulse with life

again. What had been a wasteland destined for oblivion now brims with energy. There is a playhouse, a library flanked by a casino, beerhalls, and several movie theaters. The ghosts of Bertolt Brecht live side by side with McDonald's hamburgers.

Mario Vargas Llosa once wrote, "Grosz's images will not stop haunting me this morning while Renzo Piano and I look over what was (and soon will be) Potsdamer Platz, the new cultural, historical, political, and economic center of the future capital of Germany. Here were once the cafes, galleries, theaters, hotels, upper-crust snobs, beggars, invalid veterans, elegant women, and prostitutes that Grosz painted, distorted figures marked by contrasting colors, imbued with an effervescence and muddle of tones and lines and features, images of this neighborhood that have been forever engraved in collective memory."

There was nothing left of that world; all of it had been wiped out. In Berlin they expected my father to fill a black hole.

Of course. Expectation, the anxiety of starting out. When we began work, the only residents were the ghosts of the past.

My first impression was a sense of emptiness: a few blackened walls, shaggy trees, no tangible sign of the past. An historic center with no footprint, a memorial site with no memorials. I remember the acrid smell of burnt oil from the Trabants issuing from the East. It stuck in your throat. There was an endless line of those small backfiring cars with bright, duroplast bodies.

After they tore down the Wall, not a single brick was left to commemorate what happened. They wanted to forget. They eliminated it completely, as if it had never existed.

After the war people preferred to erase rather than remember and piece things back together. It was a form of collective suppression. I think that Berlin wanted to recapture its innocence.

The city could have been rebuilt in 1945. There were ruins, remnants with which to start over, and there was time; the Wall was not erected until sixteen years later, in 1961. Instead they razed the city to the ground.

They made the shameful decision to split the city in two with a barrier, spools of barbed wire, and ditches. A place once filled with the beauty of Potsdamer became the beat of *Vopos* and wolfhounds who patrolled a constantly floodlit border. Anyone who tried to scale the wall was to be shot on sight. But Berliners held captive in the Democratic Republic concocted all sorts of escape plans: they curled up inside car trunks, jumped from windows, swam down the Teltow Canal. Some fashioned hot-air balloons with blankets, others tunneled under the Wall, and the acrobat Horst Klein crossed over by balancing on an electric wire.

The historic upheavals contributed, somehow, to the project. The client was Daimler-Benz, at the time helmed by Edzard Reuter, son of the anti-Nazi hero Ernst Reuter, the first burgomaster after the surrender.

We stop for a coffee—if you can call it that—opposite the Berlinale Palace, the new site of the Film Festival. The choreographed smiles of actors have also helped restore the desert to life.

A man in his seventies approaches our table. He must have recognized Herr Piano. After apologizing for interrupting, he asks if Potsdamer will ever go back to what it was. I think he is referring to the golden age of the *Oberkieker*, when women donned extravagant hats. My father had already answered his question, in a speech at the inauguration, which he gave in English, since he knew only a smattering of German. But Kennedy didn't speak German either, and he at least said, "*Ich bin ein Berliner!*"

I remember it was the morning and so cold that ladies were

going around the square handing out blankets. They carried trays topped with glasses of Schnapps, the one means of warming up while people on the stage droned on. When it came time for him to speak, the Constructor said, "Potsdamer Platz cannot go back to what it once was. How can you hope to reproduce those transient days? The fervor of everyday life back then? How can you reproduce the pride of building the first traffic light in history? On the other hand, this place has always teemed with life. Why shouldn't it again? Actually, it already has, just look around you. The cruelty was to have taken it away from here, the terrible cruelty of the war and the shelling.

"This place is part of myth and memory. And the memory of a city is long. Like the memory of elephants. But a long memory does not preclude the desire to forget. It is one of the paradoxes of Berlin, which is at the same time nostalgic and forgetful. You Berliners possess a cult of the past yet seek to cancel the past. In 1945 the ruins were quickly swept away. In 1989, a few months after the Wall, one could not find a single fragment of it left. Rather than bearing witness to the past, the Wall was recycled into a tourist trinket. We may have been the ones to build this square with its buildings, streets, and lake. But you Berliners will be the ones to make it a part of your daily lives, your daily rituals. The ones who bring it to life."

The man courteously bids us goodbye—the truth is everybody here acts polite out of a sense of guilt—and fades into the intensely sweet smell of the lindens. The smell brings promises of summer and settles in a particular spot of the soul.

Divers from Odessa

Berlin is made of empty space: gardens, large squares, rivers. Overhead is the sky with Wenders' angels, below an underground lake. Water is important to this project. It joins what the Wall divided. Dig a few meters down and you find yourself underwater. The whole city is built on water, this area most of all, since it is wedged between the Spree river and the Landwehrkanal, the canal where the Nazis eliminated dissidents.

In the early 1990s all the streets were lined with red and blue tubes that would pump water from every construction site and pour it back into the water table. There were thousands of them. The tubes allowed people to work on dry ground, but not us. Our site was so vast that we would have lowered the groundwater in the Tiergarten by at least half a meter and risked killing the trees. We would have been bailing water for a year and a half and pouring it out two miles away, in the plains by Tempelhof Airport. It wasn't possible.

The Tiergarten is a forest of beech trees, the usual lindens, and a few conifers. Some people lie in the park reading the *Bild*, some row across the pond, giving the water lilies a wide berth. There are fields of rhododendron, brooks, footpaths, and a white swan gazing loftily from the pond. They couldn't risk lowering the water table. They had to find a creative solution.

Something simple yet complex. If we couldn't drain the water, then we needed to work in it, to lay the foundations by descending to the bottom. So we created a large lake. I've seen everything on a construction site, but until then I had never had to use divers on dry land.

A hundred came from Holland, many others from Odessa. The men were big and burly. They would descend about twenty meters deep into total darkness. The water was so murky you couldn't see anything. They worked four hours a day in two-hour shifts. Every time they came back to the surface, they had to decompress for an hour.

In the winter the lake surface was covered with a sheet of ice. Berlin is far north, 52°31'07" North, 13°24'29" East. But the divers didn't lose heart. Actually, they were quite pleased to see the water freeze.

I remember how the Ukrainians, who were accustomed to the cold, would dig holes in the ice sheet before diving, same as Eskimos fishing on packed ice. Then they would dive to the bottom. I thought it would be a problem, but one of them explained that the icy crust was a boon, since they could quickly locate the exact spot where their colleague had stopped working. You just had to mark the ice sheet red and the next man would dive down to the same position—no need to use the GPS system, which isn't accurate to the meter and forced them to sift through muddy water. You could hardly see a thing down there.

That diver was an awesome figure. He came from Odessa, and his name was Timur. He spoke German with a thick Russian accent, and our local architect, Kristof Kolbecker, would try to translate what he was saying into English. I don't know what I managed to understand.

But the diver helped his cause by gesticulating. On a construction site the universal language of gestures is paramount. You don't need a lot of words. You catch only flashes of conversation. Timur was very proud of the work he and his companions did. That I had no problem understanding.

Every construction-site story has in common that kind of solidarity, and pride in building. That was true of the Japanese carpenter from Kansai, the Austrian mountain-climber who scaled the Shard every day, and the diver from Odessa working below the ice pack in Berlin. Building means teamwork, which is why I'll never tire of saying that it is a gesture toward peace and coexistence.

Russian Bombs

The Allied troops reduced Potsdamer Platz to a handful of dust. They dropped a surfeit of bombs on this sliver of the city. Many failed to detonate and remained lodged in the ground. Over the years many were recovered using Geiger counters, but they couldn't detect bombs more than two meters below the surface.

When you start to excavate a site, you turn up all sorts of things. One time they called me at the office in Paris. They had just begun to dig. The foreman explained that a bomb had been found in the jaws of a crusher, those machines that reduce waste materials to make concrete. It could have exploded. But no need to worry, he joked, the bomb was Russian.

Over the course of construction we found five more. They installed a small museum of bombs, grenades, guns, and helmets in a hut.

There was an important writer hanging around the Potsdamer site. Writers, like retirees, are irresistibly drawn to construction sites. Maybe because a construction site changes from one day to the next. Watching a building go up sows seeds of hope in a person. Maybe a construction site is a poem, a fragment full of promise. Or maybe writers, like retirees, have time to kill.

You know I love construction sites. They've always been extraordinary terrain for discovery.

It isn't true that a blueprint tells you everything, because it is only on the construction site that you understand the value of things and decide to attach importance to what on paper appeared irrelevant.

The man hanging around the frozen lake happened to be the Nobel laureate Mario Vargas Llosa. Back then Vargas Llosa split his time between London and Berlin. The construction site employed five thousand workers, only five hundred of whom were German. It was a microcosm of Uzbekistani, English, Turks, Italians, Egyptians, and the *marangoni* [14] from Odessa. My father counted twenty-five different nationalities. Unlike the Tower of Babel, in Potsdamer Platz everyone understood one another regardless of language barriers.

Maybe because communication served a specific purpose: They were patching together a city that had been devastated by the horrors of war with the kind of enthusiasm and pride such an enterprise entailed. Potsdamer Platz held up a mirror to a multiethnic society.

"Do you see, Renzo?" said Vargas Llosa. "This was the theater of the worst intolerance in history. Like it or not, today it is a theater of mass integration. Knowing that the future center of Berlin, this enclave that once formed the axis of the most hysterically nationalist regime in history, will be a product of cosmopolitanism, strikes me as an excellent omen for the future of Germany and makes me deeply, madly happy."

Another thing architecture can do is replace a site of intolerance with one of solidarity. Like Berlin, which went from being the capital of the Third Reich to a vibrant metropolis where, out of 3.5 million inhabitants, a million come from abroad.

One demonstration of the project's diversity was the "dance of the cranes." On October 20, 1996, Daniel Barenboim stood on the scaffold and directed Beethoven's "Ode to Joy," so that twenty

---

[14] Translator's note: Famous divers from Genoa who explored Roman ships sunk by Caligula in Lake Nemi, in the Lazio region.

crane operators, who between them spoke at least four different languages, could follow along as he waved his two flags.

I remember the rehearsals after work. The crane operators had to study Barenboim's gestures, just like musicians. They couldn't believe it. They asked questions in the most peculiar languages as they sought to understand the unfamiliar language of the orchestra director. It was a beautiful occasion. Twenty cranes danced in perfect unison to the score.

Scylla and Charybdis

The main square is named after Marlene Dietrich, dedicated to that beauty who drove away the darkness. Today Berliners are happy about the decision to dedicate it to the Blue Angel, though at first there was resistance. She was a wonderful woman and great actress yet is still considered a traitor.

Not everyone was willing to honor the diva who became an American citizen and sang "Lili Marleen" in English to comfort Allied troops at the front.

Convincing the burgomaster to dedicate the square to Dietrich wasn't easy. There were still those who believed she'd turned her back on Germany. Someone once wrote that Berlin is caught between the Scylla of self-pity and the Charybdis of self-importance. Agony on the one hand, pride on the other. These two sentiments are genuine and affect all Berliners. It's in their nature. They want to forget their terrible heritage yet at the same time mourn their past glory.

You can almost see her again, Marlene Dietrich, the singer whose voice broke your heart. With the gentle touch of her first name and the slap of her last. They all come back to me, she says in *The Blue Angel*. Even Berlin has come back to her. Right where the war had left a painfully blank slate.

But has my father fulfilled his promise in Potsdamer Platz? Did he achieve that perfect, unattainable something, that Atlantis, which, after wandering for seven months, we still haven't found?

Are you asking me if I'm satisfied with this work? Well. It's a bit repetitive, monotonous.

When you think of a design, you picture beautiful images of cities, streets, neighborhoods, and squares—full of light, shimmering with energy, life, sounds, and colors. But when you try to capture them, to make them a reality, they slip through your fingers.

The Right to Complain

We returned to Rouen, where Monet had painted the cathedral at sunrise, in broad daylight and at the end of the day. The *Magnaghi* and its crew were waiting for us there. Also awaiting us were the white sand beaches of the Mediterranean and Greece. Thinking about them takes me back to vacations on *Didon*, our old family sailboat, which my father rarely allowed us to disembark. Even at night he refused to take us ashore, unless the mistral was blowing. That was the primary reason the crew mutinied—*we* mutinied, that is, along with our mother, whom he nicknamed Didon. We slept at anchor, sheltered from storms by nearby promontories or in coves.

Any time anyone complained, the Explorer would tell the following story. During the Republic of Genoa there were two types of contracts for sailors. Those who did not complain received a higher salary, and those who exercised their right to complain, who whined, earned a smaller per diem. The majority who set sail preferred to earn less and gripe openly.

Not that they were lazy. They pulled their weight. Only to the tune of complaining. In nautical dictionaries, to complain is to quietly express displeasure and criticism of an order that is, nevertheless, followed. There was even a designated area before the topmast where people could talk trash and hurl insults. They could curse captains, shipowners, and their wives with impunity. Actually, the commanders appear to have preferred it, because that way they remained aware of any unrest on board.

According to Captain Renzo, we did not have the right to complain. (I might add we were not being paid.)

I can still see the spray on the deck, the happy faces as we set out, the tanned faces on our return, the Old Man yelling at me to fasten the mainsail. And me fumbling with the winch, and him yelling louder and louder.

There are images that remain imprinted in the neurons of our cerebral cortexes, photographs of our past that do not fade with time. The boat anchored at the Naval League in Sestri, my sister half-buried in the snow in Gran Paradiso, our dog Pippo wagging his tail at the green gate, the sandcastles we had to turn our backs on.

Our eyes aren't all we see with; we see with our memories, too. That's not just my opinion. Science has confirmed as much. Our memory stores images in the same area of the brain, the *visual* cortex, where we save the instant messages that we receive from our retina.

If I close my eyes, I can see the first sandcastle I built on Pegli as if it were yesterday. Maybe my career began there, maybe that was where I began my training. Sandcastles may not last long, but they remain a part of you forever.

15.
MARE NOSTRUM

Day 211 of the periplus undertaken by Carlo (the present author) and his father Renzo, the Measurer. We're back on the *Magnaghi*, which feels a little like home after our excursion to Berlin.

As you enter the Strait of Gibraltar from the Atlantic, the water changes. Two bodies of water merge. The warmer, denser, saltier seawater of the Mediterranean flows into the fresher oceanwater. The waves change, too, becoming shorter, smaller, more rapid. The difference lies in the fetch, the area of the ocean over which the wind blows in a constant direction and at a constant force for a certain period of time. The stronger the winds and the farther they travel, the taller the waves. In the Mediterranean fetches are not as long because the area is geographically enclosed, a body of water surrounded by land, dotted with islands and cliffs that act as windbreaks, so the winds have less room to roam. According to calculations, springs, rivers, and rains take about a hundred years to replace all the water in the Mediterranean, and no one, not even my father, can measure how much old water and how much new water it contains.

No other sea has such an abundance of sounds, legends, perfumes, history. Nor has another sea witnessed the rise and fall of so many civilizations: the Greeks, the Cretans, the Myceneans, the Egyptians, and the Romans, who called it Mare Nostrum. Meaning that, after so many conquests, the entire sea belonged to them. Some people liken it to an enormous sea sponge, saturated with experience and knowledge.

In front of us, on the African coast, stood the ruins of Carthage, the city founded by the Phoenicians, who, with their triremes and Hannibal's elephants, challenged Roman authority. Carthage is now a rich suburb of Tunisia. Before the Punic Wars, you could find Phoenician merchants in every port. Their nautical maps, the most reliable at the time, were engraved on copper plates to prevent them from eroding. They ventured beyond the Pillars of Hercules, in search of tin in Cornwall and gold on the Atlantic coast of Africa. They crossed the threshold between the known and unknown world.

When Hercules separated the Calpe and Abila mountains, dividing Europe from Africa, he inscribed on them the words *"non plus ultra,"* no farther. You could not sail beyond that point. Plato had his Atlantis, Dante his Mount Purgatory. For others there was simply the edge.

Punta de Tarifa and Point Cires are separated by seven nautical miles of choppy water three hundred meters deep. The currents of the Mediterranean are weaker than ocean currents—comparable, perhaps, to karst—in a riverbed bordered by nothing but more sea. Like rivers, the currents have a source and an outlet, though we cannot locate them. The only ones with any real knowledge of the currents are fish, who use them like a conveyor belt on their transmigrations.

Now that we're sailing through home waters and the tension has subsided, Giobatta can get back to complaining. It's about time. Cabin boys, he says, used to be forbidden to speak directly to a man of his experience. Such was the respect a boatswain commanded. Instead they would speak to an official who would relay their message to him. Back when the navy was the navy, you communicated to a man like him through intermediaries.

He talks as if he were a hundred years old, yet he isn't even fifty. He grumbles about his superiors, about the taxes taken out of his salary, about the toll of the humidity on his poor bones. He complains.

Cultural Soup

The Mediterranean is more soup than sea, its ingredients fused in the blender of history. It is a saline lake where you can hear everything, where nothing goes unnoticed. Comparable to the scuttlebutt on boats known as *radioprora*, "prow radio." Out of cigarettes? You don't even have to ask. Everyone is on the same frequency. Same goes for this sea. One summer a fire broke out on Corsica and the smoke burned the nostrils of people all the way on the island of Elba, where we used to dock *Didon*.

A pastiche of languages exists in the Mediterranean. I'm thinking of "Crêuz de mä," a song Fabrizio De André sang in Genoese. Having circulated for centuries, the song had sopped up words from Greek, Arabic, Spanish, French, and English. In Bonifacio, in southern Corsica, they still speak Zenéize, a thousand years after the Genoese settled there.

As you sail these waters, the songs of De André arise unbidden. They are the sounds of water lapping, waves gently rocking, and of the libeccio, the undertow, the shouts of sailors.

My father and De André were friends, their bond one of deep affection and few words. They were sailing companions. Like Genoa, De André was rugged and taciturn yet extraordinarily kind. Years ago we visited him at his property in Sardinia, L'Agnata, where he spent long stretches with his wife Dori Ghezzi. He had fixed up a farmhouse and was raising pigs. There was always work being done to the place. He and Dori labored like two Fitzcarraldos, moving mountains, relocating rivers, manufacturing little ponds. I remember the green scrub, his silences, the cigarette always dangling from his lips. He loved Sardinia and its wild seaside full of fish and outrageous characters.

What you hear in Fabrizio's music is the echo of the Mediterranean. A living and breathing sea, a stew of civilizations, a mix of Italian, Hispanic, Greek, and Arabic cultures. It is the voice of the sea. What you hear is the sound of a crew pulling a line aboard, fisherman hauling in their nets, fishmongers at the market.

For thousands of years the Mediterranean has stored the same images and sounds, but you need keen ears and eyes to detect them. Populations and races fused and clashed here, like, perhaps, no other corner of the world. They say there is no single unified Mediterranean culture, but many cultures. In some ways they resemble one another, in other ways they differ. But ultimately the similarities outnumber the differences.

Arion and the Dolphin

A school of about ten dolphins is playfully cutting across the bow. They come really close to the boat and, just before crashing into it, flap their fins and avoid us. Dolphins are the acrobats of the sea; there is something miraculous about the grace with which they swim. They have sonar, which allows them to navigate around obstacles, like the sonar equipment on hydrographic ships. Plutarch said that dolphins alone possess disinterested love: they need nothing from humans yet display benevolence and friendship. Dolphins even save the shipwrecked, nudging them toward the shore with their snouts. They also have an acute sense of hearing and appreciate music.

In ancient times epitaphs were written for stranded dolphins. Three centuries before Christ, the poet Anyte of Tegea composed an epitaph in which a dolphin speaks:

No more, exulting in the calm seas, shall I rise from the depths and thrust through the waves;
No more shall I rush past the beautiful prow of a fairrowlocked ship, delighting in the figure-head.
The dark waters of the sea dashed me to land and I lie here upon this narrow shore.[15]

Dolphins were attracted to the sound of wind instruments that set the beat for Greek rowers, so that, as they do today, dolphins would swim beside boats, diving, leaping in the air, shooting spray from their blowholes.

We ascend to the upper deck, where the radars are, to get a better look at the dolphins dancing. But the second in command, Elio Tamburini, orders us back down, because the electromagnetic waves are dangerous. As they say in the navy, spend too much time by radar and you can forget having children. Maybe the saying has its basis in science, or maybe it's just sailing superstition, but when you're floating about for a long time, the way you act and the shape of your thoughts change. You need to have experienced it to understand. You don't live hour to hour but moment to moment. Your life follows the rhythm of the currents, the tides, the transit of the sun, the company of bottlenose dolphins, the flight of seagulls.

"Do you know the story of Arion?" asks Tamburini. He begins to tell it: "Arion of Methymna was a composer and kithara player who bid farewell to the tyrant of Corinth and

---

[15] *The Poems of Anyte of Tegea*, translated by Richard Aldington. The Egoist, 1919 (London)

went out to prove his artistry to the world. Success came quickly, and he accumulated so much wealth that he roused the envy of the sailors carrying him from Taranto to Sicily. Once offshore, they decided to kill him and steal his wealth. But they gave him a choice: he could either commit suicide and be buried on land or entrust himself to the waves. Arion chose to jump overboard. But before he did, he sang an ode to Apollo on his kithara.

"In comes a group of dolphins. Lured by the song, they surrounded the ship. As soon as Arion dove into the water, a dolphin, unseen by the crew, caught him on its back and carried the musician to the sanctuary of Poseidon, where it died of exhaustion. Arion then returned to the court of the tyrant of Corinth, who, hearing his story, ordered his men to build a monument to the dolphin."

After a few minutes, the cetaceans thin out, slowly dispersing. Each goes its own way. You can see them vanish beneath the water. Where they are going is anybody's guess. Maybe it's lunchtime.

When you've seen dolphins at play, they become a part of your language, like the light and colors of the Mediterranean, and the pulse of the water. You carry them with you all your life.

This is Genoa, or the sea rather, a gigantic recording device that plays back forms, sounds, smells. I equate the Mediterranean with emotions, with the coves of Corsica, myrtles and strawberry trees, De André, sailing trips with Luciano Berio. All of it together.

Maltese Stone

Seagulls are also in our wake. They coast over the waves, their curved beaks pointed down, scanning the sea for prey.

They are white with dark feathers on their wings, and yellow, cunning eyes. In the *Odyssey* Homer wonders whether they land on the surface of the sea with their chests or their claws. There is no easy answer. They seem to me to enter the water differently, depending on whether the sea is flat or rough. If choppy, they dip their wings first, to keep from fumbling on their webbed feet. Whatever the case, seagulls almost always hug the water, and looking down on them from the deck of the *Magnaghi* makes a world of difference. Your perspective changes. If they look beautiful from below as they maneuver around fishing boats, from above they are even more beautiful, since they have as a backdrop the moving sea.

In Genoa all you need to do is step out onto a terrace or climb up the hill and suddenly the view changes. You observe the seagulls from above. Their beauty becomes special. Such a sight haunted Calvino, who grew up in Sanremo. He used to talk about gazing down from San Giovanni, the road he lived on as a boy. He would look down at the port, the bell tower, the buildings, the river, the public garden. For those of us from Liguria, the bird's-eye-view is fundamental.

Looking down at the sea from the mountains is also a beautiful way to see the city, a sight to store in your memory.

The Mediterranean is many things, past, present, and dreamt. Heinrich Schliemann, "grandfather" of the impostor Paul Schliemann, imagined Troy was real and then discovered it, Priam's treasure and all. The same might happen with Atlantis. Maybe the secret is not to stick your dreams in a drawer but to pursue them. Or risk them, as my father would say.

Not unless you risk your dream will it become a reality. And, once you have fulfilled your dream, you realize you have taken a step forward, and then you'll take another and another. Because the journey must go on.

As Cavafy said, you must not hurry on to your destination but learn from every situation, admire every place, and open yourself up to cultures, surprises, and encounters.

Those who return from a journey are never the same person. They come back changed.

In the heart of Mare Nostrum lies Malta, a little over 40 miles from Sicily, 150 miles from Tunisia and 180 miles from Libya. It has been ruled by Phoenicians, Greeks, Carthaginians, Romans, Byzantines, Arabs, Normans, the Aragonese, the French, and the English. Here differences have always existed. The Mediterrenean also connects the lands it separates.

More than 450 million people inhabit the coasts. Far more than the number of people who live in the United States, three times as many as live in Russia.

The name itself, Mediterranean, means "sea between lands." It is the same in all languages. In Arabic it is called *Al-Bahr al-Abyad al-Mutawassit* (the white middle sea), in Hebrew *Hayam Hatikhon* (the middle sea), in Berber *Ilel Agrakal* (the sea between two lands), in Japanese *Chichukai* (the sea between lands) and in Albanian *Deti mesdhe* (also the sea between two lands).

Architects feel a bit like James Cook, travelling through terra incognita. That is why I kid my father when I call him the Explorer. You wander the globe, encounter other cultures, seek to understand them, and study their surrounding environment and nature, culling from your impressions to build upon their foundations.

An architect trains for many years by walking the streets, talking to people and grasping their needs and desires. He learns to observe the city and absorbs all of its features.

He observes the course of its rivers, its woods and tides, the direction of the winds, the transit of the sun during the equinox and the solstices. In short, an architect labors to build in order not to seduce the world but to change it.

When you look up at this island, or islands—Malta is an archipelago—the light is dazzling. Thanks not only to the sun but to the way the stones reflect the light. The stone paints everything around it gold. The Maltese use this limestone to build everything from houses to museums to the pavement to towers and walls. It stays cool in the summer and warm in the winter months. There is an abundance of this stone along the coasts, but it is not always good for building. You need to find the right quality of stones, stones lying at the appropriate depth, stones of suitable durability.

Here the Surveyor reimagined the historic Valletta City Gate, the rampart that greets visitors and is flanked by the fortifications of the Knights of Malta. The project also entailed building the new Parliament House and restoring the ruins of the Royal Opera House, which had also been destroyed by bombing campaigns. Too bad we won't be stopping there, but the trip would take us off our course.

The local stone is the real star of the design. In nearby Gozo a quarry was reopened to provide us with the limestone. I like the idea of combining the past and the future, history and modernity, in a place like La Valletta. Preserving the ruins, imbuing them with dignity and repurposing them, reinventing old materials with modern-day science and technology.

Just as we did with the stone, which was wrought and polished by CNC machines.

Natural light filters through the buildings. That prismatic light, which changes with the winds and seasons yet is recognizable no matter where on the shore you are standing, that light Van Gogh chased after in Provence. You can never tell if that shimmering color is green or purple, can never tell if it is actually blue, because a second later it turns into shades of pink, or gray.

Paul Klee recovered his joie de vivre thanks to the color of the Mediterranean. The same light is described by Mohamed Choukri in Tangiers, Luigi Pirandello in Girgenti, Orhan Pamuk on the Bosporus. It makes the rocks of this sea glisten.

The sea is not all romance and beauty. It is also an escape. The sea entices us to get away, becomes the desert beyond which we travel to conquer our future. And when you leave and journey around the world, the sea remains trapped inside you.

The experience is so intense as to mark you forever. The harbor, the adventure, the world, and these big ships, big as whales, coming and going. The sea becomes your language.

As they set out from the harbor of Nantucket, the sailors aboard whaleboats would cry, "All around the world!"

The Mystery of Graham Island

Maybe the destination of our journey is the sea itself, what it preserves. Shipwrecks, pyramids, (practically immortal) jellyfish, as well as hard work, rainbows, dreams wandering in search of a harbor, smooth white logs floating along, mysterious islands, and desires—outrageous desires. Last year the *Magnaghi* collected data in the area around Graham Island. The island is monitored in case one day it resurfaces. On their campaign the *Magnaghi* collected fragments of rock and samples of fumarolic gases and set up three stations equipped with seismographs.

If the island still exists, it isn't far from where we are now, sixteen miles off the coast of Sciacca and twenty-nine from Pantelleria. Though the island itself has shrunk to a large sheet of rock lying a few meters underwater, it has a fascinating story to tell. Verne wrote about it in *The Wonderful Adventures of Captain Antifer*, but the island is not the novelist's invention.

In this exact spot Africa's tectonic plate collides with the even larger plate of Europe and Asia. As the plates move, they break up the earth's crust, and lava is released and hardens underwater. That was how Graham Island formed, rapidly appearing and just as rapidly disappearing, in the span of six months. In 1831, a sixty-five-meter tall mountain with a surface area of four square kilometers emerged from the depths. According to eyewitness accounts at the time, the first signs of movement were observed in June. On July 17 the island was nine meters tall, five days later it had grown to twenty-five, and in August it reached its peak.

Descriptions of the event call to mind Dante's circles of hell. Fishermen saw a bank of dark clouds accumulate and cast a purplish glow over the sea, while boiling water generated small eddies. The sky thundered, flashes of lightning illuminated the night. Columns of smoke suddenly rose, and jets of hot water shot into the air and sank back into the sea. Waves carried pumice and lapillus to shore. Fishermen reported a huge toll of dead fish. When they lifted them out of the water, the fish were "boiled, distorted, and covered in combustible material."

The new island was quick to arouse the interests of authorities and the scientific community. Sailing crews came back terrified. Their accounts filled the harbor taverns with dread.

Upon hearing these stories, Ferdinand II, the Bourbon King of the Two Sicilies, dispatched the corvette *Etna* to inspect the island, since the tiny plot of scorched earth held a strategic position. William IV of England sent his own observation ship. At the end of July the island was a small bay in the shadow of a hill. On top of the hill could be spied a smoldering lake. Naturalists said they saw turtle doves starting to make their nests.

The Bourbon King christened the island Ferdinandea and planted his flag in place of the Union Jack. The English called the place Graham Island. Theirs weren't the only flags unfurled there. There was also the French flag, carried by Constant Prévost, a Parisian geologist who named the island Île Julia.

But, due to erosion and subsidence, Graham Island disappeared in January 1832. Its sinking ended the dispute about sovereignty. To avoid any future misunderstandings, the Sicilians placed a stone plaque on the submerged surface: "This strip of earth once known as Ferdinandea Island was and always will be the property of the Sicilian people."

Today all that remains of the islet is a shoal of volcanic rock indicated on maps as the Bank of Graham. It is hard to say why this submerged rock always ends up at the center of diplomatic intrigues. Maybe because the Mediterranean has been a battleground since the time of Salamis.

Baccan Pasculli had often sailed in this stretch of the sea. He was here when people thought the island was going to re-emerge. As he tells me the story, a group of dolphins returns to follow the *Magnaghi*. "In 1986, a few months after Gaddafi launched a scud attack on Lampedusa, seismographs recorded a tremor in the exact location of Graham Island. Immediately, geophysicists at the observatory in Erice thought the island was about to resurface. They alerted us, but it turned out not to be the case. An American bomber had taken off from the base in Sigonella and was headed to Tripoli. Flying over the island, they mistook it for a Libyan submarine and dropped a few depth charges."

16.
CITY OF MUSIC

N*avigare necesse est.* The Romans were the first to enshrine into law the free use of the sea, provided one did not impinge upon the rights of others. It fell under the *res communes omnium*, the property of all, like the air and the sun, which no one had jurisdiction over. Anybody could sail and fish where they pleased, and make use of the water. The Mediterranean was transformed into a peaceful lake bustling with life, with traffic and travelers. Though it did not last long, the Mediterranean became, for a while, Mare Nostrum.

We are not going to Rome. My father is convinced Atlantis isn't there. Soon we'll pass by the peninsula of Sorrento and sail across the same stretch of sea where Homer placed the island of the Sirens and *baccan* Pasculli is hoping to test water samples. Alkalinity, phosphates, nitrites, nitrates, coliform bacteria . . .

We continue to talk about sirens. The boatswain says that hiding off the coast of Lecce is the castle of the Siren Queen, a garden of algae and coral tended by drowned sailors. There's plenty of theories about sirens. For some people they are chaste priestesses, for others they are neither priestesses nor chaste. Some believe that what gets mistaken for sirens are rogue waves that produce melodies. Some believe they are cannibal prophetesses. Still others claim they are seaside prostitutes or Sirin, half-women, half-owls from the East. Often, to placate them, a wooden figurehead depicting a siren was mounted on a ship's bow. I wonder what their songs were like.

Homer doesn't describe them. I cup my ear to catch the sound of their honeyed voices. But a disappointing silence is all that reigns, broken by waves crashing against the hull.

Yet there must be some truth to them. Tales of mermaids exist all around the world. In Japan there are the shy Ningyo, on the Isle of Man live the lovable Ben-Varrey, on the Red Sea the Memozini, the daughters of the Pharaoh Ramses. The icy Scandinavian waters are home to the Havfrue. In Brazil people venerate Iemanjà. Orejona, a figure with a woman's legs, webbed hands, and gills, swims in Lake Titicaca. Along the coast of Ireland we find the Merrows, in Thailand the Duyugun, in Java Nyi Blorong, in the Niger Delta Mami Wata, a water spirit who confers magical powers. Even in Australia they have local mermaids, the Likanaya and the Marrayka.

A Tragedy about Listening

Music has always been closely associated with the sea. Music and water are twins, both elusive, written on the same fleeting score. Both are fluid, rhythmic, and melodious. Like music, the sea is lightness, instability, song. The waves have a vibration frequency of eight cycles per second, the same frequency as alpha brainwaves. Is that why it is easier to listen on board a boat?

I was in the middle of the sea when I learned I had won the Auditorium competition. It was summer, and I was pulling fenders up into the boat at the Strait of Bonifacio, a place typically battered by a rough northerly wind. The circumstance was peculiar, because nothing has greater acoustics than a ship. It's like a sound box.

They contacted me on channel 16 VHF to say that Francesco Rutelli, then the mayor of Rome, was desperately looking for me.

I called him as soon as I was back on land; back then I didn't have a cell phone. He wanted to tell me that they had decided I would be the one to make the city of music.

My father and music have a long history. Their unreciprocated love began in high school, or thereabouts.

At school I was a dunce, as you know, but I also played the trumpet. Not half bad either. There was just one problem: I was tone deaf.

I wanted to play like Louis Armstrong and was crazy about Maurice André, too. One day Gino Paoli—we were scouts together—advised me to quit. Friendship is cruel.

After that I decided to study architecture. And, over time, I became a luthier; the Auditorium in Rome is a sound box. In Paris I worked with Pierre Boulez, who introduced me to the world of music, and two artists, Luciano Berio and Luigi Nono, who would go on to become friends for life. And then there was Claudio Abbado. Brothers in arms all.

He collaborated with Nono and Abbado on *Prometheus*, a production that placed the orchestra in a wooden ark. I remember him taking me to the deconsecrated church of San Lorenzo, in Venice, to hear it. I was probably too young to appreciate it, but the subtitle, "A Tragedy about Listening," seemed to me spot-on. He and Berio, another Ligurian, from Imperia, engaged in absurd sailing races. Berio once gave him two Maremma sheepdogs, named Cotton and Fioc (Ball). The male was a real character. For years he would bite the backsides of the architects at the studio in Vesima; architects from Japan were his favorite victims.

The violinist Salvatore Accardo is my youngest brother Giorgio's godfather. Accardo agreed on one condition: My father had to make Giorgio listen to music for fifteen minutes a day. Good music, didn't matter what kind, as long as it was good. My father must have kept his promise, for a while.

Berio was the one who demanded I enter the competition for the Auditorium in Rome. Luciano was very willful. Whatever we did together, he was the brains, I was the muscle.

Berio and the Explorer had endless conversations that I was forced to endure. Especially out on the water, where there's no escape. They were both obsessed with sound spatialization and carried on for hours about music and architecture. The immaterial art, which exists in time, and the most material of arts, which resides in space.

Music is immaterial, not abstract. Sound is air quivering in space, physicality. An architect is a constructor of music boxes. When designing a concert hall, merely achieving acoustic perfection is insufficient. An architect must also give it character. And he has to grant everyone access to the same emotions at the same time. One of the beautiful things about listening to music is that we listen to it together.

Luciano and I talked all the time about the power of tradition, the role of geometry, the nature of sound, the power of sequencing, and often, very often, about the lightness of music and the heaviness of architecture.

My father has always admired musicians. Maybe even envied them. The Auditorium itself was inspired by an image that betrays that envy, an image of a pianist playing alone, in empty space. Free of the problems associated with construction sites, heavy materials, inflexibility. The Constructor pictured what surroundings this pianist would have dreamed of being in, and then he populated it.

Yes, I envy them, first of all because they can play and I'm incapable of playing. And because music is ethereal and quick, whereas architecture is bound by the limits of gravity.

Three Beetles

My father is an omnivorous listener, hence disorderly. There's a bit of everything in his record collection: Genoese folk music and Keith Jarrett, Gustav Mahler and Georges Brassens. On his phone he has a piece by Maurice André. Every time he hears it he swoons.

Music is also the sounds of work, the sounds that serve to synchronize labor, like the trade winds blowing through the huts in New Caledonia and the sound of the horn at the steel plant in Sesto San Giovanni that announces the end of a shift. The Auditorium in Rome is a space designed by music, sound, and acoustics engineers, who measure the reverberation time with computers, lasers, and ultrasound machines.

Acoustics engineers are a cross between scientists and musicians. They work with music and love it. But computers and acoustical engineering are not enough, nor is it about having perfect parameters. The warmth might still be missing.

They say a musical instrument has character. The same is true of a concert hall. That is why I have always sought the advice of my musician friends to breathe life into the sound and give them a space where they would love to play.

Today Romans refer to the halls of the Auditorium as "The Cockroaches." Beetles might be a more elegant nickname, but that's Rome for you. The dome of St. Peter's is "The Cupolone," or Big Dome; the Altar of the Fatherland "The Typewriter"; the Christmas tree in Piazza Venezia

"Spelacchio," or the Mangy One. It's their way of showing affection.

More than anything the three halls resemble medieval lutes. They are spaces designed to create a physical phenomenon (the propagation of sound) and to act as places where listening to music is a public ritual. A sense of community is fused with the technical and scientific aspects of sound.

The (requisite) scientific approach constantly overlaps with a humanistic vision.

While we talk I catch my reflection in the water over the stern rail. The image is distorted, messy, almost cubist. Maybe mythological monsters are modeled on our reflections: tritons, sphynxes, centaurs, chimeras, harpies, flying fish. Though flying fish do exist. We came across a school of them leaping in the air off Cape Passero. They spread their pectoral fins, like wings, and their tails act like rudders, allowing them to escape predators by gliding over the water. But ichthyology is not, at the moment, a subject of interest to my father.

Because the Auditorium was constructed at a bend in the Tiber, that is where the adventure began. Archaeologists performed the necessary preliminary investigations, but they didn't fully account for subsidence: how much the ground had, for millennia, sunk. So when we began excavating we found a villa from the sixth century B.C.E that, owing to the phenomenon, had collapsed three meters. We decided to incorporate the *domus* into the complex, and now it is visible from inside the foyer.

It dates back to the age of Tarquinius Priscus, the fifth king of Rome, who had the Circus Maximus built so that the Romans could watch games and performances. It was a gift of *genius loci*, that villa.

Topos was not only a metaphor but a reality. We had to move the halls and find a way to display the remains of the villa to enable people to visit it. Today the Auditorium is more than a performance space; it is a part of the city's cultural heritage. There are shops, galleries, bars, restaurants, one of the city's most popular bookstores, and the Conservatory of Saint Cecilia. People live and work in the piazza, the Cavea. As with all cultural spaces, the Auditorium provides the city with a place where we can come together and celebrate our identity.

Berio used to say that music, like mountains, forests, and rivers, has a long lifespan. Same goes for architecture. Buildings must be lived in and enter into the rhythms and rituals of the city.

Operation Skerki

Sounds like a successful project, and it may well be. But once again something isn't quite right; the gap between concept and reality remains unbridgeable. It's like trying to catch a bird of paradise: just as you're about to grab hold of it, it always flies away.

I have often made buildings dedicated to music. The IRCAM in Paris, the *Prometheus* ark in Venice, the theater at Marlene Dietrich Platz, the auditorium at the Lingotto in Turin, the Niccolò Paganini in Parma, the Cité Internationale in Lyon. And later at the Isabella Stewart Gardner Museum in Boston and the Greek National Opera in Athens.

But the Auditorium in Rome is not just any auditorium. It is a city of music, with three halls, an outdoor amphitheater, large rehearsal and recording rooms, a ten-acre park where music resides.

But that wasn't my question. What fails to convince him?

Some critics have objected to his obvious allusions to Roman cupolas, pointing out the colors and lead cladding.

Lead has proved to be one of the longest lasting metals in architecture. It has been used a lot, including in the construction of historic buildings, from the Hagia Sophia in Istanbul to the dome of St. Peter's. I find nothing wrong with it.

My regret is another. Every hall has a different size. The largest seats 2,800, the smallest 700, and the midsize 1,200. Perhaps I should have made that difference more visible, should have made the differences in scale and function more apparent.

His dear old sense of inadequacy is rearing its head again. Some of his regrets haunt him, like the time he attempted to build a school in Costa Rica. They had even completed a final design, but they never managed to make it happen. Why it failed I don't know. My father never talks about it. All I can say for certain is that it gnaws at him.

There are projects I never managed to see through because something stopped me. They're like children that never saw the light of day. And the defeats are often bitter.

Like the school in Costa Rica.

Milly had followed that project closely and passionately. Then it came to nothing. From time to time, I still imagine that little building on the outskirts of San José. In this profession, something always slips through your fingers.

We are 470 miles from Athens, but the weather in mid April is trying. The forecast for the evening calls for stormy weather, with winds up to twenty-eight knots, and rough seas the next morning, with northerly wind speeds of twenty-four knots.

Captain Pasculli wants to change course so that he can conduct surveys about eighty miles northwest of Trapani, near the

Skerki Banks, a group of reefs that, though close to the surface, are invisible and insidious. Since the age of the Romans—the ancient Romans—all sorts of things have sunk there.

But before plumbing those depths they have to calibrate the sonar so that their measurements are precise. The speed of sound, as it travels to the seabed and returns to the ship, changes depending on the salinity and temperature of the sea. Pressure is also a factor in shifting the parameters at different depths. If the apparatus isn't calibrated, the data isn't reliable. With his assistants Mario Bentivoglio and a stout kid named Lucianone, Duccio Frascaro, the head of the hydrography division, is fiddling with the block and tackle on the stern. They lower a probe into the sea to calculate the exact speed of sound in that place, at that moment in time. Then they hoist it back up and connect it to a computer, which transfers the information to the sonar in bands.

Now they will be able to map exactly the different heights of the seabed. The same operation, referred to on board as a descent, will have to be repeated in the morning, when the water is warmer, and in the evening, around nine, when it cools after the sun has gone down.

Once again we have to place our trust in sound to continue the journey.

17.
STONE SICKNESS

The boatswain complains that we've run out of hard-tack. Once upon a time they kept hardtack in zinc-lined lockers, shielded from the damp air, from mice and cockroaches.

Sailors soak it in seawater and eat it with anchovies and a drop of oil. British hardtack was, apparently, disgusting, so tough you could chip your tooth on it, couldn't be softened with boiling hot coffee, whereas hardtack from Genoa and Odessa turned moist immediately and tasted good. But it was more expensive, and most captains preferred to save their money. Because, for one, any capital they managed to save ended up in their pockets.

Giobatta says that sailing without hardtack brings misfortune. A world of superstitions floats on the Mediterranean. Chickpea soup is a harbinger of bad weather. Abusing a seagull bad luck. Ditto dressing in green or bringing umbrellas and bananas on board. In this book of legends, the chapter on misogyny is long and would have us believe women on board augur disaster. Better to skip it.

The most widespread myth concerns changing the name of a boat. According to tradition, all ships have souls, and their names are recorded in a ledger by the gods of the deep. So changing the name is an insult to them. You can do it, but there's a catch. You have to hang a brass plaque with the old name next to the new, so as not to betray the ship's spirit. The French adopt a different strategy: they only change the name on August 15, after having zigzagged upwind and taken the same route back.

According to another superstition, you should never set sail on a Friday, because in Christian doctrine Fridays are inauspicious. But, to hear the *nostrommu* talk, it has nothing to do with religion and everything to do with the fact that Thursday was payday and sailors would return to work drunk. Leaving the next day would have been too risky.

Sailing under the blazing sun of the Mediterranean, scorching even in springtime, my father and I talk a lot. There is nothing to count or measure, the sea is choppy, and the crew has no time to entertain our questions. A lot of questions come up on board: What's a companionway? A rhumb line? What do the helmsmen mean by flukes, scuppers, snatch blocks, cleats? Nobody answers. They are too caught up with their duties.

In the Ionian Sea the waves flow south from the Strait of Otranto, which separates Punta Palascia, the easternmost point of Salento, from the Cape of Gjuhëz in Albania. For my father, the thought of the old city of Otranto releases the hatch of his memory: the old city with its narrow roads paved with stone orbs catapulted by the Turks and left as decoration, with its white houses, its baroque crests of fallen gentry, the Castello Aragonese guarding against Saracen raids.

Signorina Maroccia

Forty years ago my father teamed up with UNESCO on an experimental endeavor called the "neighborhood workshop." The idea was to rehabilitate and revive historic centers in collaboration with local residents.

As I already told you, a lot of people spend their lives persuading others of their ideas without worrying much about whether or not their ideas are right. The issue isn't convincing people. It's doing the right thing by listening and understanding. It's a delicate art. It calls for silence and slowness. Listening to others does not mean deferring to them but to making better designs based on your understanding.

In Otranto we worked with local residents on the design, deciding as a group what actions to take and trying them out. Together we opened up the construction site and monitored the job. We also implemented a diagnostic system: we explained how to look after the old walls. We treated the terrain, just as a good local doctor treats the health of his patients. It was there, in that building workshop, that we came up with idea of the archidoctor.

The idea of an archidoctor tickles the crew. It doesn't take much to make people on a boat laugh. It's one way of releasing the tension that has built up over months spent trying to shake off the waves. In the words of Baci chocolates—to which I owe part of my education—a smile is a curve that sets everything straight.

It's no laughing matter.

An archidoctor finds solutions to carry out restoration projects without forcing people from their homes, for a home is a shelter from fear and instability. You can't be so pitiless as to uproot people. People are inextricably linked to the walls that surround them. A home provides physical and psychological protection, security, and comfort. All of us, and I mean all of us, spend our lives trying to get back there.

Look for a man and you'll find a home, every time. That is why we need lightweight, low-impact construction sites that do not displace people. Of course, an operation that sophisticated takes longer to build and requires a lot of patience.

I remember a small, white, hot-air balloon set down in an equally white square where there were two poles and a tent, also white, with tables and canvas chairs. When the kids stopped playing soccer, they would come sit down, exhausted, cradling their ball, and browse through blueprints, scribbling on them with colored chalk.

The workshop was an inclusive site. Residents took pride in the old town again. Our experiments had become an attraction in the square. There were moments of real beauty.

We sent a camera up in the hot-air balloon to take aerial photographs—drones didn't exist back then. Every time the white balloon rose in the air was an event.

Hundreds of people participated in the evening meetings around the tent. They came to talk about their homes and history, the materials and architecture.

We redid the roof of Signorina Maroccia's residence. She was a kind woman who volunteered for the experiment. We ensured that her life would go on as normal while we repaired the building.

Otranto, the lightweight construction site, the archidoctor—these endeavors followed on the heels of the Beaubourg escapade. Compared to Beaubourg they were tiny. After all the polemics surrounding the *raffinerie*, no one wanted to entrust a large project to my father. It became a subject of conversation in our household. Sure, he had gained fame, but fame came with complications.

Beaubourg made Richard and me popular, though our popularity was pretty controversial. There is no denying it. It was a large, prestigious, highly visible project, but the adventure also left me in a daze. In a certain sense, Otranto helped me return to the origins of my profession as an architect: teamwork on a technical scale, the open construction site, the symbolic value of building.

Beaubourg was followed by a period of real strain. The experience had lasted six years. I had been fully immersed in that endeavor and in that city, and they left a real mark on me. I had discovered disciplines and dimensions that I had never previously encountered in my work. Afterward I felt I needed to return to a more direct relationship with the goings-on of life, I wanted to re-immerse myself in a construction site on a more human scale. During my time in Paris, I missed engaging with the community, the old city, the periphery, and small-scale construction sites.

All of those things go way back, to infancy perhaps, to the construction sites of your grandfather Carlo. So, for a few years, I worked for UNESCO on collaborative projects. I worked with President Senghor on the periphery of Dakar. I did a couple of projects with Melina Mercouri, then culture minister of Greece. One was in Crete—in Chania, to be precise, on the docks of La Serenissima, where the Venetian galleys were built—and another in Rhodes, on the ancient walls.

Craftsmanship

The mere mention of galleys is enough to revive the interest of *baccan* Pasculli. Ships, ancient ships in particular, are his domain. He speaks at length about those vessels—propelled by oars, sometimes outfitted with Latin rigs—that plowed through Mare Nostrum for three thousand years, until the advent of sailing ships, practically.

Galleys were employed for warfare and trade. Pasculli explains that the Italian word for galley, *galera*, is based on the Tuscan pronunciation of the Venetian word *galea*, the Genoese word *garea*, and the Greek word *galeos*. The name means "shark," and the boats were so called for their slender oblong shape and the naval rams on their bows. A galley's long, lean hull made it fast and easy to maneuver. But the hull was also its Achilles' heel; galleys were unstable in rough seas, and their narrow holds meant they had to hug the coast to keep their thirsty rowers supplied with water.

The captain rattled off the various types of galleys: the penteconter, the liburnian, the bireme, the trireme, the quadrireme, the quinquereme, the galliot, the fusta, the light galley, the bastard galley, the large galley, the galleass, and the galleon. But his favorite is the dromon, a Byzantine vessel whose forecastle was equipped with a primitive flamethrower that shot Greek fire, a combustible compound that could ignite on water. The fire could only be put out with urine, sand, or vinegar. Only the emperor and a handful of armorers knew the composition of Greek fire: a mix, so it seems, of pitch, saltpeter, sulfur, oil, naptha, and quicklime.

The boatswain talks right on into the evening about the *Bucentaur*, the Spanish *Real*, the *Sultan* commanded by Ali Pasha. Until my father cuts short his disquisition.

After Beaubourg, I was accused of being a technologist, of focusing exclusively on design details. For years. I didn't build Beaubourg because I'd skimmed a few books, but because my father was a constructor. A constructor with few workers but great dignity.

Growing up on construction sites leaves a deep impression. And my childhood as a little constructor instilled me with a passion for the extraordinary business of building.

Your grandfather Carlo called it stone sickness.

Hence my first works were pure experiments. I was doing things that concerned the skeleton of architecture. It was a naïve refusal of form.

I began by studying the materials, on the construction site. And

I was exploring a method of building that differed from my father's. The truth is, without craftsmanship, you won't go anywhere.

Besides, the academy is to blame for separating the moment of inspiration from the moment of executing a work of art, for this absurd approach to art as pure conception. In fact, science, reality, and the artistic emotion they produce, are inextricably linked.

I once visited Jean Prouvé's class at the École des Arts et Métiers in Paris. He handed each student a sheet of paper and a pair of scissors and told them, "With this piece of paper you have to make a bridge from here to there." "Here to there" was longer than the sheet of paper, so there were no excuses; you had to invent. Some folded the paper, some cut it, some rolled it up. Prouvé walked around room and rested the pencil on top of each bridge to see if it held. I find it a remarkable way to explain the principle of trial and error without having to say much.

Prouvé was a man of few words, your grandfather was not a big talker, Albini never spoke. So, I came to the conclusion that masters don't talk much. Actually, maybe they shouldn't talk at all. Maybe real masters lead by example alone, in an open and comprehensible manner. Such that young people can take from them and go on their way.

My father has always considered himself more builder than architect. He is usually ill at ease around his colleagues. There is Richard, but Richard is a different story. They're friends, blood brothers. They were before the construction of Beaubourg, they were during the construction of Beaubourg, and they were after the construction of Beaubourg. Even if they parted ways, both of them say there was no special reason for the separation. It just happened.

Richard wanted to return to his family in London, and my father went on to open a new studio in Paris. They continue to talk on the phone, reunite, go sailing.

I have also been criticized, ever since Beaubourg, for having no historical memory, for being a noble savage. They accuse me of being indifferent to history. They may have a point.

But things could be worse. You could be paralyzed by dwelling on the past. In any case, I've always remained outside of the clubs and academies.

Starchitect? I'll Pass

He was criticized, attacked, opposed. Like the time the prefect of Paris swore—*moi vivant, jamais!*—that he would never have spoiled the square with those gigantic ears. And now everybody praises him. There isn't a journalist around who doesn't attach the title of starchitect to his name. He hates it.

Yes, I was welcomed into the temple, but I almost prefer things as they were before. After decades of distrust, they've sort of put me on a pedestal. Everything you do is *wonderful*!

Wonderful this and wonderful that. Thank god there are still criticisms, especially irritating criticisms—the only kind that serve a purpose. Even pans can be useful, when they're justified. They beat idolatry.

Now that awful term starchitect gets thrown around. In no way is it an honorific. Quite the opposite. It casts a sheen of superficiality over you. When you become successful, you fall prey to narcissism. Everything around you becomes self-referential, no one tells you the truth, and even your drafts are held up as works of art.

The risks are great, but I developed a good habit of making ugly sketches, like writers who jot down quick, clumsy notes so as not to fall in love with them. A sketch should not be gloated over. All it should do is remind you of its contents.

18.
GINO'S WAR

I f only we could see past the sea, down to Africa and its unbroken stretches of savanna . . . But it lies beyond the limits of our vision, even with the captain's prism binoculars. All around us is water, the frothy Mediterranean encircling us as far the eye can see. We can picture the Gulf of Sidra on the opposite shore: Medina, Tripoli, and Benghazi, coastal deserts, salt marshes, the routes of camel trains branching out into the Sahara.

They say that over time the sea yields up everything, our memories most of all. Like the memory of a sunny afternoon in Entebbe on the shores of Lake Victoria. Present were Gino Strada; Yoweri Museveni, the President of Uganda; and the Explorer, wearing a wide-brimmed Panama hat. Many soldiers in camouflage were on hand, carrying assault rifles and sporting mirrored sunglasses. In nearby South Sudan, the civil war continued to rage, and every year thousands of migrants found a welcome refuge in Uganda.

About twenty women in flashy yellow tunics were clapping their hands to punctuate the president's speech. They weren't so much a claque as a bassline. They made three rounds of *clap-clap, clap-clap, clap-clap*, followed by one long *clap*, after which they held their arms out toward the speaker, inviting the public to listen to what he had to say.

Museveni has run the country for over thirty years, ever since he led the revolution that toppled the dictator Idi Amin Dada, a man who had proclaimed himself Lord of All the Beasts of the

Earth and Fishes of the Sea. There is no sea in Uganda, but for Idi Amin that detail was insignificant.

What were we doing in that distant land? The fact is, for every thousand children born, almost five hundred die of curable diseases. So, EMERGENCY had decided to build a pediatric hospital and designated Entebbe to be the site, since it was relatively peaceful and had a healthy climate. At over a thousand meters above sea level, there is less risk of contracting malaria. Entebbe isn't far from the airport in Kampala, either, so it can be easily reached by patients, ideally accompanied by their parents.

The *Magnaghi* begins to pitch more violently. Mediterranean waves are shorter and choppier than the waves in the Atlantic. Especially during this season, when the ostro and gregale winds are blowing.

Night has fallen, and it is startling to think that most of the stars we're gazing up at no longer exist. Though they've been extinguished for thousands of years, they act as our guides.

Scandalously Beautiful

What I remember most is the sunset on Lake Victoria. It lasts a moment; at the equator the sun sinks below the horizon and skips past the romantic twilight interlude. Suddenly, with no warning, it's dark.

But what does all this have to do with the Explorer? With Museveni? Tribal warfare? Children in need of care? I have an idea about what led him to design the hospital.

It all began with a timely encounter at an unhappy time. He met Gino Strada shortly after the death of Strada's wife, Teresa. My father had sent him a letter of condolence and Strada called to thank him. Gino told him that he'd had a dream of building a scandalously beautiful hospital. His words exactly: scandalously beautiful.

The scandalous idea of a free world-class hospital won my father over. A gift should be beautiful, otherwise what kind of gift is it? Especially if it is for children in need of a future.

A hospital is beautiful if you are unafraid to check your child into it, as Strada sees it. He doesn't simply want Africans to come to him to be treated; on the contrary, the idea is to bring the treatments to them, to leave them in their world during times of suffering, to entrust them to a team of local doctors and nurses. Spreading knowledge is the point, because excellence is a positive contagion.

That, too, is a form of beauty, the beauty of knowledge, of scientific curiosity and solidarity. We are all in the same boat and we all suffer the same sea sickness, whether we're on the Mediterranean, the Baltic, or Lake Victoria.

It isn't the first time that my father has worked in Africa. He often talks about a project in Senegal that never came to pass.

My experience in Dakar was wonderful and disappointing. UNESCO was spearheading an initiative aimed at repairing the relationship between tradition and innovation. In the 1960s, an aqueduct built in Dakar pumped so much water that it lowered the water table by half a meter and killed almost all shallow-rooted plants that had been used to cover the huts in the interior. The Senegalese replaced the roofs with corrugated metal sheets, so in the summer the huts were sweltering and during the rainy season you couldn't talk over the drumming of the rain. In the underground aquifer we identified plants with deeper roots, which could have replaced those previously used.

But nothing came of it. For the locals, corrugated metal roofs had become synonymous with modernity. Senghor explained that they saw those corrugated metal sheets as the pinnacle of progress imported from the West.

Architecture is dictated by necessity, true, but most necessary is the will of the people.

Maybe that was part of what attracted him to the challenge of building on the African continent. Something had been left unresolved, something that needed fixing.

The rooms in the hospital in Entebbe will face a courtyard with a grove of purple jacaranda trees, an emblem of life and healing. Convalescent children will play in their shade.

There will be eighty beds in the hospital spread out over 9,000 square meters, three operating rooms, health screening services, a blood bank, a pharmacy, a training school for doctors, and a guest house for visiting families.

Another thing intrigued my father. Actually, he had been obsessed with it since Dakar. When he met Strada for the first time in Genoa, he asked him what the soil over there was like. Strada said it was clay. Exactly what the Constructor wanted to hear.

I had waited for a long time and always wanted to use earth to make walls that protect against the heat and cold, to build a roof that harnesses the energy of the African sun. I was just waiting for the call from Gino, and one day it came.

The next day, Raul Pantaleo, an architect who has designed hospitals for EMERGENCY, left for Uganda to get a sample of the earth there. It needed to be studied and analyzed. He was stopped at customs. They couldn't understand why he wanted to board with a suitcase full of clay. The Constructor was to blame. He wanted to see it, touch it, smell it, observe its reddish color. The idea was to combine the ancient and modern, to revisit traditional local practices of kneading clay, to employ a rammed earth technique.

Maybe it was the red earth that convinced him. Maybe it

was his connection to Gino Strada. Or maybe he had been inspired by all the women you encounter on the streets down there, each encircled by three or four children, the littlest one straddling her back. Many of the children suffer from deformities that must be corrected before they come of age.

To this day, the majority of buildings in the world are made with dirt.

I was first struck by the fact that on Lake Victoria everything is red: the earth, the roads, the houses, the sunrises and sunsets. Our studies showed that the composition of the clay is good, that we just needed to apply the right methods and additives to turn it into excellent building material. The clay is extracted from below the arable layer, then compacted using a rammed earth technique. Treated with water, the mixture is then placed inside a wood formwork and later compressed with a piston.

With no firing process to speak of, this method of building with raw earth saves a lot of energy.

Earth has the added advantage of being on site: you dig and build without having to transport the material. And, given how dense it is, the soil has thermal inertia. Making sixty-centimeter-thick walls keeps the building cool during the day. Clay walls have the added advantage of being very attractive; their striations reveal the workmanship that went into them. Inside the building you can find traces of the hand that made it.

This hospital must be a model of excellent medical care and environmental sustainability. That is why we are harnessing the energy of the earth, water, and sun, resources that represent the greatest—the true—aims of modernity. Each wing will be covered with a roof that creates shade and produces energy, which is captured by over two thousand photovoltaic panels that ensure the hospital's energy independence.

Lowering the Flag

Gino Strada ministers to everyone, victors and victims. His mission is to save lives, the ethical standard for a surgeon. When doctors take the Hippocratic Oath they promise to care for each patient with equal scruple, regardless of ethnicity, religion, nationality, social status, or political ideology.

That view is shared by *baccan* Pasculli, who, before commanding the *Magnaghi*, spent years coming to the aid of boats packed with migrants from Libya who risked their lives in the Strait of Sicily. He says a sailor is dutybound to help those in danger and save as many people as possible. Personal opinions do not matter. Political decisions and agreements are of no concern to seamen.

On board the custom of lowering the ensign is observed at sunset each day. The crew stands at attention in silence. Even the boatswain, who can't stand formalities, acts impeccably. But the flag is the Navy flag, not the Italian *tricolore*. In the center sits a crest, a shield divided into four squares, each containing the coat of arms of the major maritime republics, Amalfi, Genoa, Pisa, and Venice. Above them all is a turretted and rostral crown recalling the emblem that the Roman senate used to confer on *praefecti classis*, those who were victorious in naval battles.

After the flag is lowered, the youngest officer of the watch reads Antonio Fogazzaro's secular "Sailor's Prayer." The text is broadcast over the loudspeakers on the outer deck and below deck, so the machinists in the engine room can hear. Life on board stops, the moment suspended. "To thee, O great and eternal God, Lord of the heavens and the depths, to whom the winds and waves bend in obedience . . ."

Before the sailors can return to their duties, they listen to the exploits of men who received the Italian medal of valor. For each lowering of the flag, another story is told, the reasons for receipt of the medal read aloud.

Tonight is the story of Giovanni Agnes, a chief gunner born in 1906 in the province of Pavia, who volunteered for the Italian Navy in April 1923:

> Head telemetrist of a light cruiser. After a bitter stand-off with overwhelming naval forces, the cruiser began sinking. The crew followed orders to abandon ship. But Agnes, ignoring clear risk to his own person, stayed on board to tend to a gravely injured officer. Having brought the man to safety, under major duress and severely burned, he rose above and beyond the call of duty and returned to the bridge, braving flames and explosions, to destroy secret documents left behind by a dying shipmate. At sea, his unit was struck again, their boat capsized and sank, and he was picked up by the enemy.

Words that have fallen out of fashion—virtue, bravery, self-sacrifice—are spoken. Things ended badly for Giovanni Agnes, as they do for everyone who receives the medal of valor. To help a group of his comrades escape from a prison camp, the courageous telemetrist died after climbing down a tunnel to get the air circulating again. Had he not sacrificed himself, all of the men would have died.

These kinds of stories speak volumes about war, about how, over time, allies and enemies become superimposed, get mixed up, swap places. About the futility of so much spilled blood. They say war is madness.

The Old Man also keeps silent and listens. Few of us have enjoyed the privilege of peace: it's the first time in Europe that seventy years have gone by without cannon fire. That is not the case in Sudan nor is it the case in many other places around the world. When the Explorer was little, war was being waged; Germans, Americans, partisans, and fascists were fighting in Italy.

*

Those of us who came out of the war grew up optimistic about the future. That explains why, at eighty, I still believe in the slightly mad idea that things improve over time. You dispense with the bad and you focus on the good.

Will humanity ever stop waging war? There are those who argue no, because wars have always been fought and are part of our nature. Some go so far as to suggest that war is a necessary means of curbing population growth. But just because the past and present bear the stain of war does not mean that war has to tarnish the future.

When we were in Entebbe, Strada told me that the result of every conflict he had interceded in—and there were many—was always the same: nothing but the slaughter of innocent victims, mourning, and destruction. In Kabul, he studied over a thousand medical files and discovered that fewer than ten percent of patients were soldiers. The rest were civilians, a third of them children.

In Quetta he operated on children injured by toy mines, two words that, when said in the same breath, make your skin crawl. These plastic "green parrots" packed with explosives, made to appear harmless and cute, are dropped in fields for children to pick up and play with. What happens is unimaginable. Strada told me about children being mutilated, children who lost limbs or were blinded. According to an African proverb, when elephants fight, the grass suffers.

The one truth of war is the tragedy of victims, and Strada is battling to rid the world of it. Maybe that's utopian, yet the term utopia isn't nonsense. It points to as yet uncharted territory. Besides, hadn't there once "always been" slavery?

Waganga

A few years ago my father sent me a note.

Dear Carlo,

Last week in Bern we opened the museum dedicated to Paul Klee, the great painter and teacher who died in 1940. The cost of construction was a hundred million Swiss francs. A journalist and former war correspondent from the *New York Times* pointed out that that was equal to the cost of a single American bomber mission over Iraq (explosives and fighter escorts included). I was shocked to learn that with the same amount of money you could destroy everything or build something that will peacefully nourish minds for centuries.

In the hospital in Entebbe, a large roof stretches above the earthen walls, creating shade and harnessing energy. We're talking about a suspended roof with five thousand square meters of photovoltaic panels. At the equator the sun deposits an enormous amount of energy per square meter. A veritable reservoir of clean energy, an inexhaustible resource.

The roof protrudes from the building to block the rain and create shade, like the fronds of jacaranda trees or the brim of a Panama hat. The approach is scientific: a roof that converts sunlight into electricity, world-class surgeons, clay that keeps out the heat.

This kind of beauty also endeavors to combat science's sworn enemy, superstition, still present in many regions of Africa where witch doctors wield a lot of power; the population listens to and fears them. People turn to witch doctors, known as *waganga*, for several reasons: love, money, fertility, vengeance, health.

Faith in witchcraft is more popular than ever. Miracle herbs, hallucinogenic potions, ritual mutilations. Waganga cast spells on anyone who goes to a doctor for treatment. They are hostile to medicine and progress, which threatens their livelihood and power.

Yet another reason the hospital in Entebbe is scandalously beautiful: it is an island of science in a land plagued by occult beliefs.

EMERGENCY's pediatric center is a promise of beauty. It embodies the kind of global alliances that hold the world together. Our planet is not distinguished by conflict alone. Solidarity, love, scientific inquiry, sustainability—these are global alliances that unite people around the world.

They emerge here and there, sometimes shyly, traveling from continent to continent. They signal hope. And perhaps they constitute one of the forms Atlantis takes.

19.
THE FIRST TIME

The Greeks have sailed this sea, with its iodine and salt smell, for thousands of years.

We are en route to Athens, passing Cephalonia, Zakynthos, where Calypso Deep, the most cavernous abyss of the Mediterranean, plunges five thousand meters. Then it's on to Patras, the Corinth Canal, the breeze bearing the scent of wild herbs, and Salamis Island, where the ghosts of Themistocles and the Persians still clash.

To the Greeks, the sea was never just a battleground; it was also a site of contemplation and poetry. *The Iliad* opens with a fitful Achilles looking out at the vast stretch of shore being lapped by the waves. *The Odyssey* is the archetype of the seafaring tale, and Odysseus the embodiment of a sailor. He was also skilled with an ax, able to chop down trees and construct a raft in a matter of days. Almost better than our Giobatta.

Before setting out on a periplus, sailors would stop in Delos to consult the oracle of Apollo on the smallest and, thanks to the radiant scales of mica in its rocks, most luminous of the Aegean Islands.

If the oracle said it was safe to go on, then the sailors would stock the cargo holds, unfurl their sails, and launch out. Auletes were also brought on board: the sound of their wind instruments set the pace for oarsmen and attracted those melomaniac dolphins. The Greeks never—or almost never—settled anywhere farther than a day's walk from the coast, because they needed the Mediterranean. The heroes of myth were expert swimmers and fearless divers.

It was a civilization founded on the sea. They had different words to define it: *Pontos* was the sea on which one traveled, *pelagos* the high sea, and *als* conjured the image of a salt-encrusted expanse. *Thalassa* was the most generic name. By *kolpos* they meant the area that hugs the coast and by *laitma* the deep sea, the dwelling place of monsters.

Lightbulb

But *anoxis*, an ancient word that has survived into modern Greek and now means spring, may best explain how the sea was a guiding principle of Greek life.

The season we've been experiencing these last few days of April, almost eight months since leaving the port of Genoa. It feels like a lifetime ago, as if I were another person, a distant relative to myself. After sailing so long, I find everything—my past, my father, and his past—appears different. The prism of travel takes apart your memories and rearranges them.

Originally, *anoxis* also meant the moment a ship sails into the open sea, as well as the moment when your mind grasps an idea for the first time. When the cartoon lightbulb goes off.

Yes, because there is a first time for everything: the first time an idea came to you and the first time you realized it. I can clearly recall my own first time. I must have been eight years old and was sitting on the wood table in the attic of the house in Pegli, on the fifth floor.

I had built something that by a miracle stood upright, and my older brother Ermanno walked by and said, "Well done, Renzo." You always need somebody—a parent, a sibling, a teacher—to tell you "well done," to give you a push. After which you have to learn to reassure yourself.

It is still that way. I still find myself turning something over in my hands and being shocked to discover I made it. How you arrive at an idea is mysterious, and it is extraordinarily satisfying when that idea leads to something you can hold in your hands.

Just like I wrote in my birthday letter.

Thanks, from Renzo

What letter? I never heard about a letter. On the day of his birthday we were crossing high tides in the Cape of Good Hope. All I remember is clinking glasses with *baccan* Pasculli and the other officials in the mess. That's it.

We had fetched a bottle of aged grappa from the pantry for the occasion. No speeches, just a happy birthday with little fanfare, as is the custom among sailors. And now I'm learning that my father had sent a message to his team at the studios in Vesima and Le Marais.

He hands me a sheet of paper scribbled all over in green ink. Just as the *Magnaghi* prepares to enter the Corinth Canal, a cut in the rocks so clean it's as if a gigantic scalpel had been taken to it. Sheer, ninety-meter-high walls loom over our heads. But passing through this isthmus relieves you from having to sail around the Peloponnesus and shaves 135 miles off your route.

I read the Constructor's letter. Maybe he wrote it to put his architects at ease about his having up and vanished. They must have wondered where he'd gone. Subject: *Thanks, from Renzo*.

Friends,

Today is an important day. Incredible as it seems, I am turning eighty. I was born on the exact day I always wanted to be born, September 14, 1937, in the last century. Eighty years is a long time. Taken one by one, the years go by slowly. But as soon as they're past, they disappear all of a sudden, in an instant. The most important thing I have to say to you, even if at the moment I am in the middle of the ocean, is that you are my birthday gift. You, who make my days so rich, intense, and creative. Creativity is a miracle as long as you know how to share it.

Our office is a special place where that miracle happens every day.

Thanks.

The other thing I have to say is that I will not retire. Not because I am charitable, but because I like what I do too much. Besides, architecture is the only thing I know how to do.

I'm not retiring because it takes a lifetime to build all this. It's too wonderful a profession to leave behind.

Have you ever asked yourselves why it's so wonderful? For one, it's the profession of building. We like crafting well-made things.

We build shelters for people: museums, libraries, hospitals, concert halls. Public places, where people with the same core values gather.

But we are not just builders. We work for the common good, a largely forgotten concept that still exists. We're not moralists but architects of moral character.

There is something else that makes this profession noble and extraordinary. The pursuit of beauty. The word is hard to articulate. As soon as you open your mouth, it flies off, like a bird of paradise. Beauty cannot be caught, but we are obliged to reach for it. Beauty is not neutral; pursuing it is a political act. Building is a grand act, a gesture toward peace, the opposite of destruction.

Friends, it took many years to arrive at this point. And do you know what helped me get here? A little device called a hidden compass. A hidden compass enables you to stay on course or, when you drift from it, to get back on course.

One last thing. Our profession involves creativity, which is the art of sparking new ideas. But where do ideas come from? My question is for everyone, especially the youngest among you.

Ideas come because at a certain point you find the courage to have them.

I would like to make a suggestion: Try, friends, go out on a limb, take a risk. I'd like to hear one of you in a meeting ask, "Can I say something stupid?" Aim to say something more than just stupid, why not.

Don't be afraid to take a risk and don't get offended if someone stops you. Be that courageous.

What makes our office special is, I think, the freedom to speak up. Exploit that freedom, take advantage of it.

Remember when you were kids and you succeeded in making something for the first time. Remember the wonder and surprise of embarking on a creative life.

Friends, take a risk. At first our ideas for designs come to us that way, almost silently. Then someone seizes on them and carries them forward. One passes them on to another, the other takes them no questions asked, and goes on his way.

Creativity consists of such courage. Rediscover your childhood, adolescence, youth. That is why I am grateful for you, and the reason I am not quitting. The kind of coherence I am talking about is what the French call *fil rouge*, a common thread. It must be pursued. Every so often the thread gets tangled up, and you have to search for it again.

The common thread is what makes a life coherent. It can snag and waver but, in the end, it goes on.

He had signed the letter in green, unsurprisingly. Out of curiosity I flipped through a handbook of color psychology: "People who prefer green want to see their opinions prevail and see themselves as arbiters of basic and immutable principles.

They put themselves on a pedestal and tend to lecture others. They want to dazzle, crave attention, and need to have things their way no matter the objections or general resistance." Make of that what you will, reader.

Shocking Anna

But is there really a common thread that connects my father's childhood sandpiles to the Shard and the "flying" canopy of the Niarchos Foundation?

My father remembers watching the miraculous birth of a freestanding wall at the start of the 1950s, the magic of seeing something emerge from nothing. After which he grew up obsessed with the idea of a job well done, convinced that a job requires a certain amount of time. Otherwise it will turn out poorly, ugly even.

His thinking aligns, to a degree, with the ancient Greeks, who drew no distinction between what is good and what is beautiful: you couldn't have the one without the other. As a consequence, a good job is a beautiful job. But maybe his real *fil rouge* lies in building places for people, in the heroic enterprise of building better places.

Many roads lead to becoming an architect. You can arrive by way of poetry, history, sociology, or construction. I arrived by way of construction. I didn't even think of myself as an architect. And, seeing as my father built with brick, gravel, and cement, naturally I built with steel and glass.

As a child I experimented by taking apart everything I could get my hands on: radios, record players, fans. I rarely succeeded in putting them back together. I would conduct my tests on the terrace, which, along with the attic, was my favorite place. At the top of the stairs, beside the door, was a storage closet, one meter and twenty centimeters per side, which served as my workshop where I kept all my tools. There was a whole world up there on the roof, my land to conquer. My mother would rather we were on the terrace than playing in the street. That is where I spent my days. I couldn't have been older than ten.

It overlooked the sea, in full sunlight. At that age, in your head, you accumulate the images and light that you will carry with you for your whole life. You accumulate a trove of shapes, emotions, and fantasies that never leave you. And you must mine that trove all your life. They are your roots.

I made all sorts of things on that terrace, structures that survived no more than a few hours in the wind, and I built crazy machines that required electric wires to run. Whenever my contraptions stopped moving, I would send my sister Anna, who was three years younger than me, to check on them. She was blonde, I remember her as being beautiful. If she got shocked, it meant the current worked; but it was only 125 volts and she wasn't in any danger. It was a gesture of affection, and she played an important role.

I'm not sure Aunt Anna sees it that way. She has never said anything to me about it. All she would say, with thinly veiled pride, was that for years she was the victim of her brother's engineering experiments. She would laugh about it. My father was stubborn. When he failed at something, he'd try again. Not that much has changed. Just look at our irrational journey to Atlantis.

But my favorite place was my father's construction site. Day after day I would watch in awe as his buildings grew.

That's where it all started. I was destined to be a builder. My father was a builder, as was his father before him. My uncles were builders, too. The postwar period was a time of rebuilding, and there was a lot of work in the construction industry.

Uncle Felice had a company in Coronata. Uncle Ottavio was also a builder, as was Uncle Giuseppe, who moved to Spain. Following in their footsteps was natural. I was like someone who grows up in a circus and knows he'll be an acrobat.

My father, a builder without a degree, dreamed of having a son who one day became a builder with a degree, an engineer. But even though I was happy at home, I am a contrarian by nature, and I wanted to get away, to break free.

Growing up around the sea you get the urge to run, to go on adventures and discover new lands. So, I decided to leave Genoa to study architecture, since the closest schools were in Florence and Milan.

The news came as a shock to my father. He looked at me and said, "Why on earth would you want to be an architect if you can be a builder?" He didn't understand, it seemed restrictive. In a way, he was, at heart, an architect, engineer, and builder, all in one.

In the end he was happy about my decision, but I still remember when I brought him to my first construction site. It was a tensile structure. He smoked his pipe in silence and watched me fumble about. On the drive home, I asked him what he thought. "*Mah*," was all he answered. *Hm*.

I remember it as if was yesterday. *Mah*.

Maybe he was wondering whether that flimsy device would ever stay upright.

My father left Genoa to study architecture in Florence, his first choice. But he didn't stay long.

Florence was too pretty. Its perfection was paralyzing. So, after drawing every palazzo and cornice, I asked myself, "What now?" I preferred imperfect Milan to too-perfect Florence. Milan was far less beautiful a city, but, at the start of the 1960s, far more interesting, bristling with energy.

Do you remember, in Via Carlo Valvassori Peroni in Lambrate, when I used to put you under the drawing-board lamp to warm you up?

Of course I don't. I was a few months old, still in diapers, when I was shipped off to the Po Valley.

I know my mother used to push me around Lambrate in a stroller clad in a scarf. Because I was frail and she was afraid I'd get sick from the cold and smog. According to other sources, she did it because I was too ugly, and she wanted to keep me hidden. That strikes me as being a bit of a stretch.

There was a line of poplars. And the theater of the railway station out our window. I spent my days at work and my nights at the university. Endless arguments. There was Camilla Cederna, who used to bring us chocolates. There was social anxiety, protests. There was the city. It was there that my aspiration to create spaces where people lived in harmony was seeded.

His legendary first assignment for Albini was to draw all fifty thousand cobblestones covering the "parvis" of La Rinascente, the department store in Rome, one at a time.

It isn't a fabrication. I did draw those blocks, one at a time.

I started working for Albini in 1960 and stayed on for three years, absorbing as much as I could, keeping my eyes wide open.

To get myself hired, every morning I would drop by his office on Via XX Settembre. His secretary would kindly let me in. "You again, kid?" she'd say. After a time, Albini heard me out and took me on as an apprentice in his bottega.

For that is what he practiced, the old idea of the bottega, begun in the Renaissance yet totally current, where knowledge is imparted by example and practice in the discipline.

At a certain age young people learn not by studying but by borrowing, absorbing, even stealing.

I am convinced that the bottega is the one place to communicate your experience to others. Albini believed that too. He was an extraordinary artisan. He had me do everything in his studio, including take apart all kinds of devices.

Later on, as my mother said in her letter, we wound up in London. That I remember, especially tussling with English kids. One of them, a kid with carrot-red hair, would kick me when no one was looking and then hide behind the teacher's skirt. And I was the one she would scold.

With the support of my brother and father, after graduating I was able to conduct my experiments with lightweight structures, materials, and technology. What I got from my father was spiritual, from Ermanno concrete. Ermanno let me experiment with structures and gave me confidence.

That was when I made my first workshop experiments in shell structures, tensile structures, complex shapes, and the use of wood and synthetic materials.

Italian critics and academics always regarded that work as mere technical research, outside the realm of art.

So I picked up and went to London. I loaded you, your brother, your mother, my equipment and our luggage into the Fiat 1100, and we left.

Richard was in London, and he and I began our adventure. I started teaching at the Architectural Association School in Bedford Square. I showed students how to make joints, how to put together different parts. In the morning we would make little buildings in the park and in the evenings we would disassemble them before dark.

He was training to build community shelters, places intended for people. In a way, he was following the example of the ancient Greeks. Whenever they landed on a new island, the first thing the Greeks did was choose the proper site for the agora. They would construct the city outward from there. Building the theater and temples was always the first step.

They had houses to build, a harbor pointed away from the wind, stores to keep provisions, but the agora, the place for people to congregate, always came first. Because the agora was the heart of the polis, the birthplace of democracy.

20.
EUREKA

C urrent position: 37°57'5" North, 23°34'0" East.
Day 237 of the periplus undertaken by Carlo (the present author) and his father Renzo, the Explorer.

We are headed not to the seaport of Piraeus, where ferries depart for the Cyclades, but to Phaleron, Greece's major port three thousand years ago.

The soldiers bound for Troy set sail from Phaleron. They assembled their fleet of triremes in these shimmering waters. Each boat had a crew of two hundred men, double the number of men serving on the *Magnaghi*. It was the dawn of seafaring, the period *baccan* Pasculli studied at the Naval Academy in Livorno. A galley was run by five officers: the trierarch (commanding officer), the *kybernetes* (in charge of cruising safety), the *keleustes* (in charge of the training and morale of the crew), the *pentekontarchos* (purser) and the *prorates* (bow officer).

All that remains of Phaleron's past glory is a small marina for yachtsmen. Overlooking the port is the cultural center of the Stavros Niarchos Foundation built by my father.

I am connected to this place by a somewhat uncanny incident. A few years before Andreas Dracopoulos called me about the project, Jean-Louis Dumas and his wife Rena invited me to go boating in Greece. They were my clients for the Japanese headquarters of the Maison Hermès. Milly, Giorgio, and I were on our way to meet them at the port. Our taxi was speeding along when we were stopped by the police, in the exact spot where the Niarchos Foundation now stands. We sat there for at least a half hour, long enough for the officers to issue the taxi driver a speeding ticket.

While we waited, I took a look around. Unbeknownst to me, I was making my first visit to the site. There wasn't much to see. It amounted to a large abandoned lot, which had once been the Athens hippodrome.

Was it a sign? Perhaps, since a few years later Dracopoulos, the grandnephew of the shipping tycoon Stavros Niarchos, hired him to combine under one roof the opera house, park, and national library. Besides, this is the land of omens: to know the future, ancient Greeks would solicit prophets, search the sky for signs, and read into the flight patterns of birds. Long before Bauman's "retrotopia," long before nostalgia became our prevailing cultural condition, humans were vexed by the future.

The most famous oracle was the Temple of Apollo at Delphi, on the slopes of Parnassus. Each side of the temple was inscribed with one of the four maxims on which the Greeks based their idea of beauty. The first said that beautiful are the just. The other three advised people to respect limits, shun hubris and do nothing in excess. The Greeks were so convinced that beauty was born of virtue that they carved their belief in marble.

Not only is this building important because its construction created jobs for 1,500 people, which, given Greece's financial turmoil at the time, was in and of itself a brave and positive thing. There's more. An impoverished country has special need of hope, of places to congregate and cultural centers. Of beauty. That is the most genuine spirit behind artistic patronage. Such beauty, for the ancient Greeks, is not understood as aesthetic and superficial.

The phrase *kalòs kai agathòs* means "beautiful and good," tying ideal beauty to ethics. So much so that they were joined together to form a single binding adjective, *kalokagathòs*. So when I say beauty I mean exploration, curiosity, solidarity. I'm thinking of the Platonic idea of beauty and goodness as being one and the same. That kind of beauty has the power to transform people.

I reaffirm it, we must reclaim it, they robbed us of it. When you talk about beauty today you think of cosmetics. But in Italian we say "*una bella persona*" and intend a person's essence, not just their looks. We talk about a "*bella azione*" and mean a generous and courageous act. We say "*bell'esempio*," "*bell'idea*," "*bel gesto*." The same concept extends to every Mediterranean language; "*lindo*" in Spanish and Portuguese, for example. The English use the expression "beautiful mind" to describe an intelligent person. Senghor, the poet and president of Senegal, taught me that the same is true of African languages. In Swahili they say "*nzuri*," in Zulu "*kuhle futhi kuhle*."

It's a model of beauty I came across in Istanbul and Lebanon, and it is the definition of beauty that I feel is the least elusive, that doesn't bewilder me. Because it is connected to the idea of *utilitas*, to meeting the needs of people and their desires. Beauty and goodness: needs and dreams traveling in tandem.

The Explorer pulls out the last slip of paper from his pocket, a passage from Plato. Him again, the one who invented Atlantis. The land Poseidon enriched with fountains and orchards. Shielded by tall mountains from the brisk northern winds. In its two centers sat temples and gardens, stables, gymnasia, and hippodromes. It was a rich city with marvelous architecture. And it was also good, governed justly and honestly. But when corruption, thirst for power, and greed became rampant, the city was punished and swallowed by the sea.

Beauty cannot exist in the absence of purity.

According to the machinist's mate, Carmelo Gibilisco, in

Sicilian a good dish is called "*beddu*." Only when well prepared are cannoli *beddu* and caponata *bedda*, he says.

I read the passage by Plato:

> So the mathematician or the enthusiastic cultivator of any other intellectual pursuit has to pay his debt of physical exercise by attending the gymnasium, and someone concerned with developing his physique has to compensate with exercises for the soul by addressing all kinds of cultural and philosophical pursuits. There's no other way for a man to come to have a genuine claim to both the two epithets 'beautiful' and 'good' at once.[16]

Plato is speaking about *kalokagathìa*. Beauty is not just expressed by what things look and feel like, but by what they imply and what you scarcely intuit. The soul is beautiful.

Especially here in Greece. This project places importance on public works: the national library, sustainability, the studies for alternative energy resources, the large park.
But it also conveys a sense of hope, expectation, and beauty.

Heading up to the building, we cross the new park, which stirs with spring. Cicadas and crickets are competing, like two choirs. The cicadas chirp while the crickets stridulate with bewildering force from olive and juniper branches. Even a trained ear has a hard time distinguishing between the sound of homoptera and the sound of orthoptera.

How such tiny insects manage to make so much commotion is a mystery. You can't even determine whether it is song, noise,

---

[16] Plato, *Timaeus and Critias*, translated by Robin Whitfield (Oxford World's Classics, 2008)

or language. Some say that the meter of Greek poetry, with its iambs, dactyl, and spondees, derives from listening to cicadas and their interpolations. Every time I hear them I think of Montale's "Meriggiare pallido e assorto": "To watch beyond the leaves the pulsing / sea's flakes / as the cicadas' nervy buzz rises / from bald peaks."

This hill, which grew up around the cultural center, is suffused with the smells of the Mediterranean: lemon, lavender, rosemary, myrtle, figs, tamarisk. And olives, the plant that paints Mare Nostrum best. The olive tree marks its borders, down to where its knotty trunk takes root. The hill in Kallithea speaks Greek.

Kallithea

Right, this neighborhood, only a few kilometers from the center, is called Kallithea, meaning beautiful view. But over time, despite the promise of its name, its natural beauty eroded and the panorama became obscured. The Port of Phaleron was buried, and the view of the sea was swallowed up by buildings and a gray ribbon with six lanes.

But today there is this artificial hill, whose gentle slopes have restored the enchanting Aegean to the landscape.

We wanted to make a square where you could see Athens and the sea. During my first visit to the site, years after that chance taxi stop, we went up to the terrace of a nearby hospital, slowly, floor by floor, to figure out the right height for the hill. No studies, no calculations.

We climbed up and took a careful look. The terrace on the tenth floor was the perfect height, thirty meters high.

Perfect because, from that height, you had the city on one side and the sea on the other. From day one we came up with the idea that, by raising the ground toward the sea, we would re-establish the belvedere of Kallithea.

That is how this sloping park, which gets gradually taller toward its southern end, slowly becoming steeper, came to be. Without realizing it, visitors climb thirty meters high and discover a new connection between with the city and sea, one that for decades had been erased by myopic city planning. Our first undertaking had more to do with topography than with architecture.

To cover the entire available surface with vegetation, we came up with a simple solution: we raised the ground and placed the opera house and library below the artificial hill. The project grew out of a series of questions concerning heights, proportions, and slopes. We worked hard: the slopes are not consistent, but they form one continuous path that, as you go along, is never at an angle of more than five or six percent. The walk is half a kilometer and can be covered in fifteen minutes without having to catch your breath. You climb up slowly and take in the scents of thyme, lavender, sage, and other Mediterranean flora.

Faliro Bay was once fed by the Ilisos and Cephissus rivers, whose names sound like music. There was water everywhere, then the rivers were diverted. Maybe that explains my father's idea to place a canal beside the building and parallel to the hill, where people can go canoeing and race small sailboats. The saltwater channel is four hundred meters long, thirty meters wide, and one and a half meters deep. A prelude to the sea: not quite the sea yet, but a welcome outpost for those looking to escape the heat of the city.

There was never any question about the hill and the presence of water. About everything else, yes. That is as it should be, because, in my line of work, it is easy and sometimes even comfortable to fall in love with an idea. When what you ought to do is take up the challenge of doing research.

Even the most seasoned thinker can take a wrong turn, which is why you are dutybound to question and test yourself. Creativity involves various contrasting senses and sensations: harmony and tension, slowness and speed.

In Latin there is a saying, *festina lente*, "make haste slowly." Whether or not he is aware, my father follows the adage whenever he opens a new construction site: hanging about, listening to people and the suggestions of the stone, soaking in the spirit of a place. But right now he fails to listen and plows ahead with his reasoning.

The third element we immediately thought of was a square, the heart of the complex. Inevitably, we called it the agora. An agora is not just part of the urban landscape but a metaphor for pulling together. The word *agora* comes from a verb meaning "to collect," "to gather." The forty-square meter agora leads to the theater and library.

People come here to stroll around the hill, unwind by the canal, listen to music, and study in the library, and they collide in the agora, the fulcrum of the project.

The Flying Carpet

We are on the roof of the Niarchos Foundation, where people are prohibited from setting foot. But an exception is made for the building's architect. To reach it you have to pass through the open interior of the roof, climb over joints, squeeze past a web of metal struts, and scale stepladders.

There is a whole world inside the roof. The columns holding it up distribute the weight to the entire structure by way of a mesh of beams and cable rods. It's like crossing a jungle. The system enables the canopy to move without breaking, in case of an earthquake.

On the roof we find ourselves in the middle of a sun-drenched square paved with photovoltaic panels. We are standing in the center of a large lens that absorbs the red-hot sun.

Our eyes roam over the squat white homes spread out under our feet, their chimney caps sparkling and turning in the wind. Have you ever seen the chimneys in Athens? A whole field of propellers spins and flashes in the rays of the sun.

Out at sea the silhouettes of islands can be spotted, slowly fading until they vanish altogether. They are the specks of earth that form the Cyclades, scattered in a circle around Delos. Aegina, Syros, Kea, Tinos, Ios, Naxos . . . Their names, too, sound like notes on a score.

There is a mysterious story buried in this sea, and not just your everyday fairytale. Sixteen centuries before Christ, there was a terrifying eruption on Santorini, and the caldera now crowded with tourists is nothing but the crater left behind after that long-ago cataclysm.

What we see are the remains of a much larger island once known as Thera. It was disemboweled and flooded by the sea. A jet of ashes and hot gas reached the stratosphere. Its rumble could be heard from Egypt to Scandinavia. A mantle of white tephra still covers the land.

The explosion also generated a two-hundred-meter-tall wave that crashed into Crete and put an end to the elegant Minoan civilization. That was when the myth of Atlantis was born and passed down by word of mouth until Plato put it in writing.

We have yet to find the perfect city. We did not find it in Japan, nor at the mouth of the Thames, nor even on the Isle of Pines. There was no trace of it in the Seine, nor on the banks of the Hudson or the lake in the bowels of Berlin. So we are strolling on top of this roof, continuing our search. That is the reason we are on this ten-thousand-meter wide, ferrocement flying carpet that protects the building from the blinding light of the sun. And we still go on searching.

Yes, we are on a flying carpet hovering above a building that sits on top of a hill. If you think about it, it's a natural and childlike gesture. When you design a building here, the first thing you think of is how to protect it from the sun. Not just from the heat, but from the blinding glare of such powerful light. And what's our first instinct when we want to see far into the distance? To shield our eyes with our hand.

The idea to make this canopy satisfies two functions: to create shade and to capture UV rays. The roof is a hundred meters long and a hundred wide, seventeen meters above the hill which, with a hectare of solar panels, produces two and a half megawatts, enough to meet the basic energy needs of the cultural center. It is a single block of ferrocement and, at its core, a machine that captures the sun's energy.

The light pours in from the south and casts a glare all the way to the open sea. At first you just barely make it out, then all at once the blue opens up before you. It stuns and surprises you.

Turning around, you see on the other side, in the foreground, the white web of Athens, and farther on the Acropolis, solitary, emerging behind Kallithea. In Genoa the sea lies south of the city, too, creating a special effect, for the sun causes the light to ripple; its rays hit the water and reflect back toward the city.

Atlantis

Down below, the Parthenon looms over the white valley. Its fifty Doric columns, two meters in diameter, are almost the opposite of the thirty slender steel beams supporting this roof. The Parthenon doesn't look like a ruin. It is solid, intact, robust. You get the impression that it will survive the wear and tear of the world. Le Corbusier called it a sovereign cube facing the sea.

Someone else once wrote that the Niarchos Foundation was a contemporary Parthenon.

Oh, there's no point in competing with the classical world. I'm eighty years old. At my age one has eyes to see. And recognize his shortcomings. At eighty years old one has done many things, if not the right thing yet.

There comes a time in life when accepting your powerlessness, even some of your defeats, is an honorable exit. As long as you exit with levity, almost dancing your way out, singing your song of freedom.

It takes a lifetime—and a long one if you're lucky—to learn, to understand, to put all the pieces together. Perhaps to make a building that marries people's desires with the constructor's invention and the poetry of spaces. And in order to do that you need to have been a curious child, a restless adolescent, an industrious adult.

You need to have known a lot of people, to have walked many places in silence. You need to have traveled, suffered, read many books, enjoyed many friendships and, maybe, stolen some of those friends' ideas. To have been moved by beauty, outraged by injustice, terrified by war. You must do all of that in order to then forget it, until all you are is memory.

And then, by some miracle maybe, you succeed in making the right building.

What if the search for Atlantis were nothing more than the search for beauty? A profound, secret, and unattainable beauty. Beautiful as the north star is to a sailor: unreachable yet still the star by which to navigate.

To discover, study, comprehend things is one aspect of beauty. You cannot do without knowledge; hopes and dreams cannot be stifled. Could that be the beauty that makes us better?

Many questions remain unanswered.

What inspired my father to embark on this periplus around the world? What led me to tag along? What is this desperate search for beauty?

Beauty is what we saw in the waning moon over the Andaman Islands, shimmering on the waves in the Gulf of Mexico, where albatrosses land to catch their breath after having crossed the ocean. The albatross is beautiful, shaking off the water, flapping its wings over the crests. Beauty is the north wind that pitches the seafoam in the air so that, for a second, it lights up like a rainbow.

Beautiful the oleanders, agaves, and pomegranates. Beautiful the musical huts with their ancestors' *flèches faîtières* looming above them.

Beautiful is the helmsman tying a bowline knot. That any knot can be untied, just as it was tied, is beautiful.

Beautiful is the construction site with its variety of workers, where people come together to build.

Beautiful are the lines on the *nostrommu*'s face, carved by the sun and wind.

Beautiful is our ship, the *Magnaghi*, and beautiful is its motto, *Nauta pro nautis*.

For Sappho, beauty was the moon. For the Spartans, dying for one's country.

Beautiful are the red earth of Lake Victoria and the black women dressed in yellow. The women especially.

Beautiful is the Ukrainian diver leaning on a ledge of ice as if he were leaning against the lip of a pool.

Beautiful is the *baccan* listening in silence to the sailor's prayer, beautiful the dolphin pirouetting in front of the prow. Beauty lies in the gesture.

Beautiful is this space, its crowded agora and its roof that turns the blinding light of the sun into energy.

And beautiful are all things created by intelligence and craft: Brunelleschi's cupola, an engine that doesn't pollute, a vaccine, or a hidden compass that, without fail, guides a ship north.

Perhaps beauty and goodness can go back to being synonymous. As in the days of *kalokagathìa*, the words should be pressed together to charge beauty with meaning. Beauty will not rescue us unless we rescue beauty, but beauty fades if you don't rescue it yourself.

Ithaca

Maybe this is beauty, Atlantis surfacing every so often, flickering on the horizon. A moment later you look again, but it has already faded.

Atlantis may never have existed, but you find it everywhere: in the country house where you spent summers sledding down the fields on a sheet of cardboard; in the first time you saw *Venus de Milo* at the Louvre or heard Vivaldi's "Spring"; in the rice pudding your grandmother Elsa used to heat on the stove for you; in the second time you saw *Venus de Milo*.

The search for beauty cannot be stopped, though it is best to take the journey slow. Best to meet more and other people, encounter unexplored worlds, try *bougna* and sailors' hardtack.

That is why we have crossed so many bodies of water, walked so many lands, spent so many days at the mercy of the waves or mired in *macaia* sick to our stomachs. More than eight months have gone by since we left the Calata degli Zingari in Genoa, our home made of stone and water. It seems like a century ago. It may well have been.

Real beauty is when the invisible becomes visible.

When the essence of things sprouts on the surface. This idea can be applied to art and nature as well as to science and society. Beauty is a moving target; it eludes your grasp. Yet if you define it as the Greeks did, everything becomes possible.

Like Atlantis before it fell to corruption: a city that cannot be found, a dream of perfection that, in all likelihood, you will never achieve, because your reach is too short. But you must go on pursuing it. You must go on probing the dark. I realized that there is no island of Atlantis, just as there is no perfect project, no perfect piece of music, no perfect film, book, person, or community. But it is a worthy pursuit; it is in our nature to search for Atlantis. Which is why, though we have yet to find it and even if it does not exist, I will go on searching for it.

We chased after it in the Sea of Japan, in New York, in the fickle skies of London, in the square of the Blue Angel, sailing across the Mediterranean. But what counts most is the journey. I'm continuing on.

That explains why the second in charge, Tamburini, is balancing the brass compass on the map. He is tracing our route to Ithaca, the island with the fountain of Arethusa, jagged with bays and inlets, the island Odysseus kept rowing toward. The hero spends the entire *Odyssey* tormented by his desire to see it, and then, when he finally does reach it, wants to leave again. His lust for knowledge lands him in the fires of Dante's hell.

Without Ithaca there would be no odyssey, just as we would never have set out on our journey had the Explorer not been dogged by Atlantis. For a second, from the hill of Kallithea, we caught sight of it on the horizon, a blur between the sea and sky, before it dissolved into an illusion again. Was it Atlantis? It was, without a doubt.

And it will be on my mind forever, even if it keeps eluding me. There is nothing to do but chase after it, tighten your grip around it. Meanwhile my father is measuring the height of the shrubs on this Greek-inflected hill. The shrubs grew ten centimeters taller in less than a year.

Making buildings with an attention to this kind of beauty transforms cities into better places, places that humanize life, places where life becomes civil, *urbe* becomes *civitas*.
The better the city the better its citizens.
Such beauty is one of the few things that can change the world.
For Dostoevsky's Prince Myshkin, it can even save the world.
Like the Prince, I'm inclined to think that beauty can save it.
And will, one person at a time.

I am glad I followed the Explorer: Atlantis has given us the gift of this journey and, before that, the impetus to weigh anchor. Had we actually discovered it, we may never have learned what it had to teach. It has taught us that you must set off down a long road marked with new experiences, adventures, changes of heart. There is no point in hurrying; draw it out as long as possible. Like Ulysses, an old man who has traveled up and down by the time he sets foot on Ithaca.

Ithaca sits at 38°21'57" North, 20°43'7" East. We'll have to slip past the white walls of Corinth again and sail under the bridge of Poseidon, which links Rio and Antirrio. The connecting power of bridges is beautiful.

Then we will sail on to the Echinades, the islands at the mouth of the Achelous—Oxeia, Makri, the deserted island of Vromonas—until we reach safe harbor at Vathy. Then we'll weigh anchor the morning after, accompanied by the complaints of *nostrommu* Giobatta and a good portion of the crew, who have been brooding on *nostos*, on the return home.

By now it is clear to all but one of us that we'll never find Atlantis.

The mood on board is mutinous, but nothing will come of it. They are naval men: exasperated by the distance from their loved ones and capable of breaking a rule or two, but not of betraying the flag flying at our stern. I have watched them stand silently during the lowering of the flag; mutiny is not their style.

The head chef, Savasto, requested and obtained shore leave after his wife complained to the Admiralty about his prolonged absence. I don't blame her. The cook has three kids at home, the youngest of whom was practically a newborn when we left on our periplus.

One hundred forty-four miles separate us from Ithaca. In good weather and with the wind at our backs, the trip would be less than two days. It took Odysseus over ten years, ten years of having to outwit the Laestrygonians and the Cyclops. But he was young, clever, and brave, whereas the Old Man is, more than anything, stubborn.

Does he want to be sure Atlantis doesn't exist? It wasn't in the "friendly" Indian Ocean, in the wild Pacific, in the majestic waves of the Atlantic. What is he expecting to find in the Mediterranean? We've scoured every corner of it. What are we going to do on Ithaca? Let's go back home. Don't you miss Punta Nave?

Yes, son, I miss it. But I am looking for Atlantis.

ACKNOWLEDGMENTS

The authors would like to thank the following for their collaboration: the Italian Navy, Magda Arduino, Daniela Balbi, Giorgio Grandi, Shunji Ishida, Francesca Manfredi, Lia Piano, and Consuelo Reinberg.

About the Authors

Carlo Piano, the son, journalist. Curious explorer of cities and their customs. Author of books on urban hinterlands. Loves the sea.

Renzo Piano, the father, architect. Has built in cities all over the world. As recounted in this book, his profession is one of adventure and exploration. Loves the sea, a passion he shares with his son.